THE OAKWOOD PRESS

The Malta Railway

by
B.L. Rigby

THE OAKWOOD PRESS

© Oakwood Press & B.L. Rigby 2004

British Library Cataloguing in Publication Data
A Record for this book is available from the British Library
ISBN 0 85361 621 3

First Edition published 1970
Revised Second Edition published 2004

Typeset by Oakwood Graphics.
Repro by Ford Graphics, Ringwood, Hants.
Printed by Cambrian Printers, Aberystwyth, Ceredigion.

Dedicated to the

Citizens of Malta GC.

Title page: A Beyer, Peacock locomotive emerges from the Mdina tunnel as it arrives at Museum with a rake of five carriages. Mr Nicholas Buhagiar, who was Manager of the Malta Railway from 1897-1924, is seen second from left on the platform.   *J.E. Swann*

Published by The Oakwood Press (Usk), P.O. Box 13, Usk, Mon., NP15 1YS.
E-mail: sales@oakwoodpress.co.uk
Website: www.oakwoodpress.co.uk

Contents

Mr Nicholas Buhagiar had these large urns for flowers made in 1912. Dozens of them were distributed around the upland stations. This one is seen at Attard station. The horse and cart give a good idea of scale.　　　　　*A. Pisani*

Foreword

My book *The Malta Railway* was first published by the Oakwood Press in 1970. There were many pleasurable moments at that time, not least of which was the privilege of meeting Mr R.W. Kidner.

Now, more than 30 years on, I recall that in the early 1930s as a young soldier serving in Malta with my regiment, I walked the line from Valletta to Museum (with the exception of tunnels and the odd embankment) when the infrastructure was still in reasonable condition and one could still 'feel' the line. I sometimes wonder if I am the only person alive to have had that experience.

In subsequent years I found myself, as a soldier, stationed for varying lengths of time in many countries of the British Empire and its succeeding independent countries. I saw a huge variety of railways, nearly always the work of British civil and locomotive engineers. I would mention just one of these, namely the line that ran the length of the Khyber Pass from Peshawar to Landi Kotal. In just over 20 miles there are four reversing stations, 34 tunnels and some 90-odd culverts and bridges.

Why do I speak of these railways alongside the Malta Railway? It is simply because I realised over those years that a railway line was more than its component parts. Professor Jack Simmons and Mr Gordon Biddle have written in their introduction to *The Oxford Companion to British Railway History*:

> No one can fully appreciate railways accurately and fairly, without a good understanding of how they work in all their many and varied aspects, what has governed their development and the impact they have made.

The endearing little Malta Railway established itself as one of the many links between Maltese culture and way of life, and that of their friends from other countries, including the British. The Strickland family is an outstanding example of the Maltese-British dichotomy. Sir Gerald Strickland, who was Prime Minister of Malta from 1924 to 1932 had roots in the family seat Sizergh Castle in Cumbria, a family that has given distinguished service to the State over many centuries; but he was also the 6th Conte della Catania and his mother was Louisa Bonici Mompalao. He is buried in the family vault in Mdina cathedral. His daughter Mabel Strickland founded *The Times of Malta*. She died in 1988 and lies alongside her father.

Sir Gerald, it is said, viewed the Malta Railway in the same light as he viewed a branch line in England. His last years in office coincided with the decline of the railway. He was saddened by this, but was well aware of the economic developments governing the decline.

I would suggest that anyone interested in the railway should also seek out some other books. A splendid start could be made with *Malta and Gozo* by Robin Bryans. Quentin Hughes, an SAS officer in World War II, was Professor of Architecture in Malta (1968-1973) and published books in 1969 and 1974 on architecture, especially the development of the fortresses. He was appointed an Officer of the island's Order of Merit.

The Malta Railway sits well in this august company. It also has a proud place in the pantheon of steam locomotive railways.

Chapter One

Early Days

Latest Intelligence. Malta - February, 28: The railway from Valletta to Città Vecchia in the centre of the island, was opened today by the Governor, accompanied by a distinguished party. (The London *Times*, 1st March, 1883.)

When the period of British occupation and rule in Malta began in 1800, Great Britain realised that it was necessary to introduce new methods of accumulating wealth in the islands. The last years under the rule of the Knights had encompassed several disasters, not the least of which were insolvency and aimlessness of purpose.

In 1801 Malta was declared a free port and the economy also received considerable help from the circumstances of the Napoleonic wars, although there was a temporary setback because of a disastrous plague in 1813. As mercantile interests enlarged and strengthened, and as Malta's importance as an entrepôt increased, so there sprang up a specifically 'town Maltese' ranging from the dock labourer to the merchant and financier. These groups concentrated in the area of Valletta (built by Grand-Master La Vallette in 1506, an eminent Knight-Hospitalier, after the defeat of invading Turks in the previous year) which included in its conurbation the later townships of Sliema and Hamrun, spilling over into and coagulating with the old Three Cities. It was in this area, as we shall see, that the railway had the main part of its line, but it also reached out into the areas of the 'country' Maltese, the casals and farms whose historical capital was Mdina.

These 19th century economic and social developments served to exacerbate the traditional opposition between town and country Maltese, the villages of the latter even being referred to by some as the places of the 'real' Maltese. But the farmers were by no means left out of the improvements in the economy. The long-established staple cotton industry died out during this century and the farmers substituted the growing of foodstuffs for that of cotton. There was in consequence more trade and general contact between town and country, but communication was difficult when produce could be moved only along localised, haphazard rough-strewn roads. From 1801 until the late 1830s, economic development, although persistent, was slow. By 1840 things were looking much more prosperous.

The Crimean War added to this prosperity and by the 1860s shipping tonnage was beginning to reach significant proportions. Before the opening of the Suez Canal the P&O shipping line opened a railway linking Alexandria with Suez, which helped the Maltese economy. With the opening in 1869 of the Canal, Malta's economy entered a new and special phase and the years from 1870 to 1890 are sometimes called the 'Golden Years'. This latter period of prosperity was largely due to the great increase in the amount of shipping in the Mediterranean, there now being traffic from Australia and the Orient as well as from Russian and the Danubian Black Sea ports.

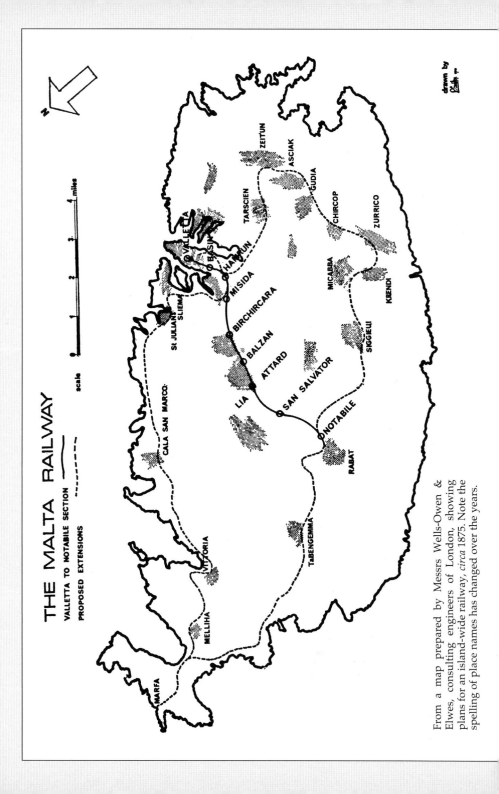

THE MALTA RAILWAY

VALLETTA TO NOTABILE SECTION ———

PROPOSED EXTENSIONS ‑ ‑ ‑ ‑ ‑

scale

N

drawn by

From a map prepared by Messrs Wells-Owen & Elwes, consulting engineers of London, showing plans for an island-wide railway, *circa* 1875. Note the spelling of place names has changed over the years.

It was of course inevitable that the Golden Years should inspire the construction of engineering works. Two of the most important of these were the laying down of a main sewerage for the Valletta conurbation and the building of a railway.

By the 1870s ambitious railway plans were being drawn up and surveys carried out. Today it might seem unnecessary to contemplate the construction of a line within such a small area. But of course our scales of time and distance are very different from those in use in Malta in the 1870s. A citizen of Valletta wanting to go to Notabile (Mdina) in the days before the railway, perhaps to pay a courtesy call upon one of the aristocracy living in the distinguished old city or to attend a religious festival, faced a 2½ to 3 hours' journey by horse carriage costing 7 or 8 shillings. The railway, smooth and rapid, was a vast improvement upon carriage travel and very much cheaper. The tramcar and motor coach were as yet undreamed of.

In the first few exciting months in the life of the Malta Railway people wrote of the countryside through which the line passed in such a way as to give the modern reader an impression of considerable distances. They spoke of valleys, fields, villages and farms through which the trains travelled. But the final total length of line was only about 7½ miles and thus it remained for the 50 years of its life. Incidentally, in the early days the Maltese called the trains 'il-Vapur-tal-Art', the 'landsteamer' and not the 'iron horse'.

It had originally been intended that there should be a network of lines giving a comprehensive service to the island of Malta. An undated map prepared in the offices of Messrs Wells-Owen and Elwes, consulting engineers to the Malta Railway Company Ltd, shows the extent of this network. The map was probably drawn up, after much preparatory work, in the early 1870s.

It shows, in addition to the Valletta-Notabile line, a proposed branch off from this line, at Hamrun, down to Tarxien, then sweeping round the western outskirt of Zejtun, through Ghaxaq, Kirkop, Zurrieq, Qrendi, Siggiewi and so on to rejoin the main line again at the Notabile terminus. This main line was to be extended. Leaving Notabile it was first to skirt round the walls of the old city in the valley round the north-facing ramparts, then on across the rolling countryside of the western side of the island to Ghajn Tuffieha and subsequently across the neck of Mellieha Bay to Marfa, the embarkation point for Gozo and Comino.

Returning again to the original main line, the northern coast of the island was to be served by a branch setting off from Msida through ta'Xbiex and Sliema, around St Julian's Bay and St Paul's Bay and thence through Mellieha to link with the line coming up from the west coast inland from Mellieha Bay. Such was the proposed general plan.

In addition it was proposed to give the city of Valletta what amounted to an internal service. There was to be an underground section from the existing Valletta terminus opposite the Grand Opera House to a final terminal under the palace at Queen's Square. From Hamrun also a line was to dip down to the waterside at the head of Marsa creek and then run alongside Grand Harbour towards and almost as far as St Elmo Point, possibly again with underground portions where necessary. This latter extension was doubtless with a view to establishing a direct link with the busy shipping world then, as for so long, the most prominent feature of commercial life in Malta.

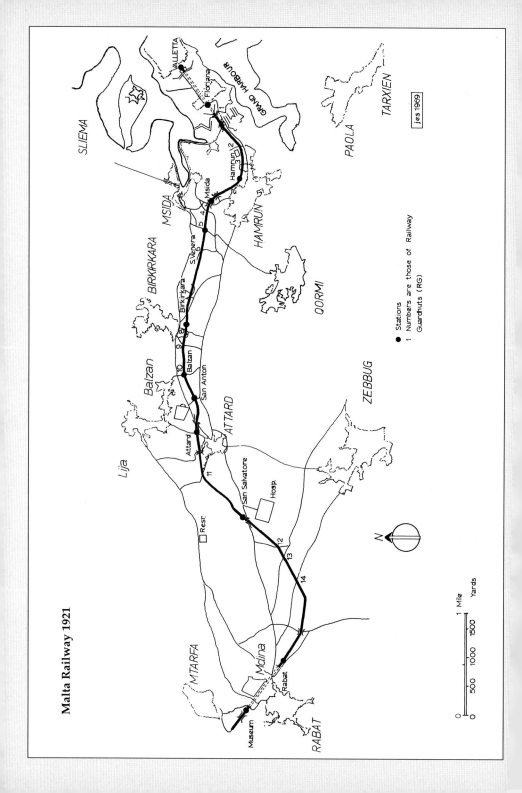

Malta Railway 1921

A 'Malta Railways Company Limited' was registered in London under the Companies Act 1862, on 30th March, 1876.* It had a capital of £1,000 in 50 shares of £20 each. It was stated that,

> ... the Board of Directors shall and such Board are hereby authorised from time to time, to make and issue and accept or indorse in the name and on account of the Company, such bills of exchange and promissory notes and other negotiable securities for the payment of money as they think expedient . . . and the Manager in Malta of the said Company shall for the purpose of providing funds there for paying the contractors and generally for the undertaking of the said Company draw bills in Malta and other places on the said Company . . . Mr Xavier Mancardi shall be the first Manager in Malta at a salary of £500 per annum. He shall be removable only on the resolution of the Company or the Directors.

He apparently never assumed office.

At their offices in Victoria Street, London, the company held an Emergency General Meeting on 15th May, 1876, when a special resolution increased the capital of the company to £100,000 in 5,000 shares of £20 each. At a further Emergency General Meeting, held on 8th November, 1877, it seems the name of the company was changed to the Valletta and Notabile Railway Company Limited, but subsequently it was dissolved.

Meantime on 12th June, 1879, another company, the Malta Railway Company Limited, had been formed. There was obviously a lively general interest in the possibilities of railway construction in Malta and equally obviously people of some inexperience became interested in the various proposals. This, however, was a reflection of a contemporary tendency to 'rush in' on railway development. A private company of this sort would have to carry out negotiations with the Home Government, Colonial Office and the Government of Malta, and as we shall see certain conditions regarding financial arrangements were laid down by the Government of Malta. Although the Malta Railway Co. Ltd succeeded in opening up a railway in the island, it had a life of vicissitudes, several changes of London address, a number of Directors coming and going, a handover to the Government of Malta in 1891 and a winding up in 1905.

Contemporary editions of *Bradshaw's Railway Manual Shareholders' Guide and Directory* give a description of the company; it had a capital £60,000 in 6,000 shares of £10 each, bearing a guaranteed interest of 5 per cent during construction, with borrowing powers. A concession for the construction of a line from Valletta to Notabile was granted for 99 years by the Government of Malta. The line commenced in the centre of the city, opposite the Grand Opera House, and passed underneath the fortifications by a tunnel 1,000 yards long. It continued 6 miles and 5 furlongs across the island, through or near the towns of Msida, Cermi, Birkirkara, Balzan, Lia, Attard, Zebbug, Musta, Nasciar, terminating at the city of Notabile, and served 100,000 inhabitants, or 15,094 per mile of line. The cost of the railway, equipped and delivered to the company in complete working order, amounted to about £10,000 per mile. The line was opened throughout on 28th February, 1883.

---

* P.P. Castagna in his *History of Malta*, 1893, p.186, says (translated), 'The railway was suggested to the Council of the Malta Government by a certain English Company - the General Works Company from London - 1873'. He is probably referring to the Malta Railway Co. Ltd. Discussions could have begun by 1873.

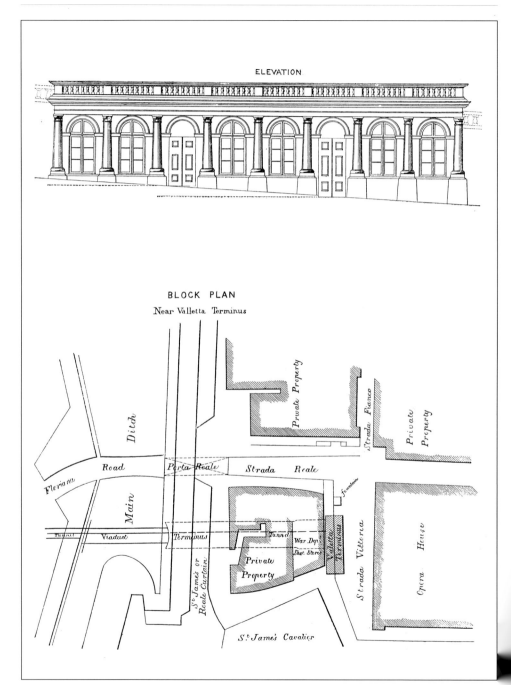

Extract from *The Engineer* showing plans of Valletta station, 13th April, 1883.

The Malta Government reserved the right at any time after 15 years from the date of opening and upon giving six months' notice, to acquire the railway, at a price equal to 17 years' purchase of the net receipts of the company upon an average of the three years next preceding the giving of such notice, with 10 per cent added for the compulsory purchase. There was a provision that if the average market value of the capital of the company during the said period of three years should exceed the price to be ascertained as aforesaid, the Government should pay a sum equal to the amount of such excess by way of addition to that price.

The Chairman was George Cavendish Taylor, who apparently took over in 1883 from the original Chairman, T. H. Hicks Bartlett. The name of George Cavendish Taylor also appears amongst the Directors of the London, Chatham & Dover, the Halesowen, the Mersey, and the Varna Railways, and it is presumed there was only one person so named and so engaged.

Although the London, Chatham & Dover Railway was aware that he had died in 1889, the Malta Railway apparently was not, and continued to publish his name in the *Manual* for some little time after his death. Indeed, had it not been that the Government of Malta took over the line at the beginning of the 1890s this un-Mark Twain-like information would presumably have continued.

The railway began with great enthusiasm and promise on 28th February, 1883, but its life as a limited company was to prove a short one. However, for the moment everything was promising. The spirit of enthusiasm attending the opening of the railway can best be appreciated by a study of the pamphlet by E. N. Zammit which was issued at the time.* It includes the following:

> A tremendous step forward has at last been taken. New economic and social horizons are opening before us: horizons so deep and wide as to effect all of us in our interests and our enterprises. The future shapes of our towns and villages are also dependent upon these movements. We largely owe this rosy future to the Malta Railway Company Limited which yesterday formally opened its magnificent Valletta-Notabile railway line.
>
> On the morning of February 28th, Monsignor the Archbishop Count Scicluna accompanied in procession by many Canons of the Cathedral and by other ecclesiastics and laity of his Palace and Curia left the Church of Victory for Valletta Station. There, in the presence of Mr F.A.B. Geneste (General Manager), he bestowed heavenly blessings on the work that had been done. Afterwards. accompanied by about sixty of the clergy, by the Reverend Mother of Sliema Convent, Mrs Geneste, Mrs Maudi, Mrs Galizia and Mrs Laferla, His Grace boarded the train, blessing the work as he travelled from station to station.
>
> The distinguished company from all walks of Maltese life present at the opening included His Excellency Sir Arthur Boston, His Grace the Archbishop, Sir Ad. Dingli, members of the judiciary, the Heads of many Government Departments, the Director of Public Works, the Press and Ladies. The engine and some of the first-class carriages were decorated with flags, streamers and sprays of tree foliage. The whole picture contributed to the general air of festivity and happiness. By three o'clock the guests had occupied the eight beautiful first, second and third class coaches. [Second class was later dropped. The newspaper report incidentally says 'two engines and seven coaches'. The explanation of the differences probably lies in the fact that two engines, Nos. 1 and 2, 0-6-0 Manning, Wardles, were fussing about and in the general excitement no one was quite sure how many locomotives and coaches actually made the trip. The photographs taken at Notabile on the opening day show what appears to be two locomotives and eight coaches.]

* 'The formal opening of the Malta Railway', E. N. Zammit, 1883, copy in the possession of Professor J. Galea MBE, and now translated from the Italian.

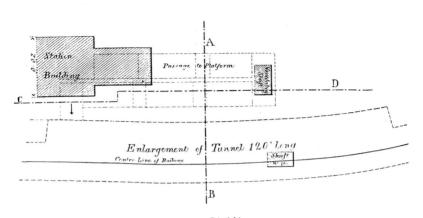

PLAN

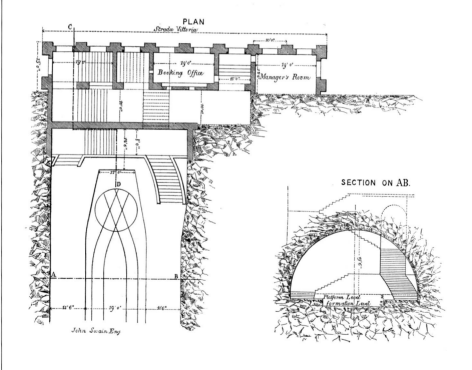

Extract from *The Engineer* showing plans of Valletta station, 13th April, 1883.

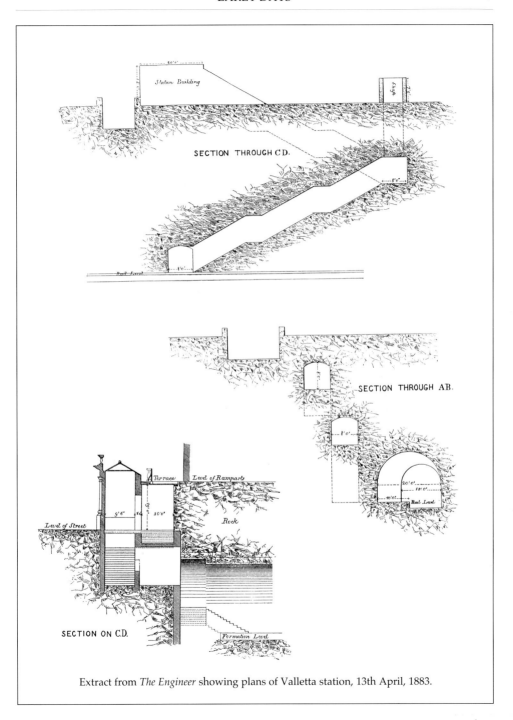

Extract from *The Engineer* showing plans of Valletta station, 13th April, 1883.

Train at Notabile station on the opening day, 28th February, 1883.

One whistle, another, then another - the clanging of the Valletta station bell - a creaking of wheels - a jolting of coaches - a rhythmic, even and monotonous rumbling - and the train drew out of the ancient capital of Malta, penetrating the darkness of the tunnel excavated beneath the fortifications of Valletta and Floriana. Huge crowds assembled at the gates of the Capital and at vantage points along the line. There were frenzied cheers for the triumphant conclusion of the building of the line. The festival spirit was abroad. The passage through the tunnel lasted about two minutes. Then, emerging into the light of day the train continued on its way amidst the applause of a crowd tightly packed all along its triumphal route.

The lay-out of the line is superb and the scenery is varied and picturesque. Now, at the beginning of Spring, there were smiling green plains, neat white cottages, and around Msida, Birkirkara, and Notabile lovely little valleys and olive groves, recalling scenes enjoyed in other lands. From Notabile the Great Port could be seen, seemingly very near when viewed from the Island heights. The train arrived at Notabile at 3.25. Its public reception was a warm and happy one. The people were there to acclaim this new link with the capital. Beneath a marquee on the hillside behind the station, the Company entertained the guests to an excellent meal.

His Excellency the Governor proposing the health of Mr Geneste said: 'Suffice to say that Mr Geneste has brought us here safely, speedily and comfortably from the centre of wonderful Valletta to the foot of this ancient Capital of the Island so rich in historical memories; and if the original founders of the Capital could take a look at that engine, I can imagine the consternation they would experience in making a comparison between the express locomotive of modern science and the slow and toilsome traffic of former times, of which we can still observe mysterious and interesting records in the multiple wheel-tracks deeply marked in the solid rock all over the island.'

Mr Robin Bryans in his charming book *Malta and Gozo*, published by Faber in 1966, says of these tracks:

South of Boschetto lies the now famous concentrations of these tracks which the Maltese call Clapham Junction . . . I found these Stone Age remains delightful, for I imagined the people dashing elegantly about all over Malta and Gozo in perhaps something like the Irish side-cars . . . I could not believe they were quite such dull things as cart-tracks . . . I like to think that these rails were connected with sun-worship, or the divination of the Stars, or for rituals now irretrievably hidden in mystery. . .

The Governor's speech also made reference to goods traffic. In fact the line was never used for goods traffic, but parcels were carried, as also was some mail. Ballast wagons and platelayers' trolleys were to be found on the line; but there were never any goods trains or goods wagons as understood in British locomotive practice and performance.

At 4.11 pm the train set off on its return journey, arriving in Valletta at 4.33. The line has nine stations - Valletta, Floriana, Hamrun, Msida, Birkirkara, San Antonio, Attard, Salvator and Notabile. These are united, to form one single station, by means of telephone wires, using a method perfected by Brequet of the Compagnie Internationale des Téléphones whose representative in Malta is the energetic and enterprising Car. Edward Rosembusch, CE.

The island newspaper report (3rd March, 1883) of the opening included the following:

The hour fixed for the departure of the opening train was 3 pm, but long before that time traffic on Porta Reale bridge was almost wholly impeded by the immense number of people who had assembled there, the walls and bastions around being also crowded with people anxious to catch a glimpse of the first train with its distinguished passengers. At almost half past two those who had been favoured with cards of invitation began to arrive in large numbers and the station presented a busy and imposing appearance. The train was drawn up alongside the platform and consisted of two engines tastefully decorated with flags and evergreens, the drivers and firemen sharing the festive appearance by having evergreens stuck in their caps; seven carriages were attached, three composite carriages with accommodation for first and second class passengers and four third-class carriages which were appropriated to the requirements of the passengers being regularly labelled for the representatives of the Naval, Military, Clergy and Civilian communities, the passengers finding their seats without the slightest difficulty or confusion.

And so the railway began its working life. The timetable at the opening showed seven trains during the day from Valletta to Notabile and seven in the reverse direction with additional early morning trains from Valletta to Hamrun and return (once) and Notabile to Hamrun (once).

Very soon, however, there were financial difficulties. Castagna, writing in the early 1890s, says that at the beginning the takings were encouraging, amounting to £50 to £60 a day, but as time passed these dropped to about £13 a day. He estimates that in its seven working years the company lost £80,000 and adds, '. . . the engines were in such a poor state that they had to be sent to the dockyard for repair and the company incurred a debt of £4,000. The engines had frequently broken down; once there was a breakdown in a tunnel and this evoked widespread protest.'

Further, says Mr L. Gatt (first Government manager of the line) rather sourly in 1893, 'the working expenses of the line are much smaller than those incurred by the company . . . the company had a General Manager at £660 a year; a Superintendent of Traffic at £350 a year; another superintendent of locomotives; ten station masters, two guards, two gangs of workmen . . . and other labourers.'

Why did the takings drop in this way? The great majority of passengers presumably were travelling in connection with their work. Was it possible that the figures reached a final level of less than £20 per day? In later years they did, although the Prospectus pointed out that the line ran through a catchment area of some 100,000 people. Alternative modes of travel were very limited indeed.

The financial facts were inescapable. Government took the matter to the courts and as a result came to own the railway in accordance with the conditions of the contract; and they were still anxious to see a successful railway in Malta in spite of the disappointments of the first years. A vigorous programme of expansion and improvement was launched and on the 25th February, 1892, after having been closed since 1st April, 1890, the railway began to run again; and now it was to run for another 39 years before coming abruptly up against crushing opposition from new means of transport.

Chapter Two

The Line from Valletta to Museum

The line climbed all the way from Valletta to Museum (so called because it was located within a short distance from the Roman Museum, an institution attracting many visitors; but also known as Imtarfa) rising in rather more than seven miles from about 100 ft above sea level at Valletta to nearly 600 ft at Museum. The sand-box was much used. On some occasions there could be considerable slipping in either direction, especially between Attard and Museum, and there is an old driver's tale of the train from Notabile which overshot Attard by many yards, all wheels locked.

The metre gauge track was single throughout, with the exception of special track arrangements in most of the stations, in sheds and at workshops. The railway did not possess a turntable and the locomotives did not all face in the same direction. Presumably, therefore, the direction in which an engine faced on track upon assembly after arrival was the direction it faced for life. The locomotives were disembarked at Marsa, packed for assembly as was usual with British locomotives going abroad. They were then taken by road to the Hamrun shops for assembly. They faced as follows: smokebox facing Valletta Nos. 2 and 8; smokebox facing Museum Nos. 1, 3, 4, 5, 6, 7, 9, 10.

There was one semaphore signal at Hamrun. Some sources say there was a second semaphore signal at Birkirkara. But Mr E.J. Farrugia, driver for many years, says there was only one - at Hamrun. There was no train staff or similar system, the control of traffic being by telephone.

There were no gates at level crossings; but there was an official known as a 'catena' on duty at each important crossing whose equipment included a guard hut, white and red flags and lamps and two chains with appropriate stanchions let into the roadside, each chain being stretched across the road on either side of the line when a train was crossing and placed trackside when it was not.

The station at Valletta was well below the street level. *The Engineer* for 13th April, 1883, reported that 'military and topographical conditions alike required that the level of the rails at the terminus should be some 35 feet below the level of the street, hence it was necessary to design an underground terminus'. Some 60 years later the 'military requirements' foresight was to be fully proved when the adjacent tunnel served as an important air-raid shelter. A writer in 1927 captured the atmosphere of the place when he said 'it occupies a peculiar if not unique situation, in being located partly in a tunnel excavated in the rock beneath the St James's Curtain of the stupendous fortifications - anciently the bulwark in Europe between Christianity and Islam and which rises in places to a height of 250 feet - and partly on a masonry viaduct, constructed in the deep moat of the fortress'. (This viaduct was originally timber.)

The plans for Valletta as prepared by Messrs Wells-Owen and Elwes show that at street level (almost opposite the Royal Opera House) a station was built which owed its inspiration to the classical Doric. The railway company obviously felt that their building should match in dignity the immediate

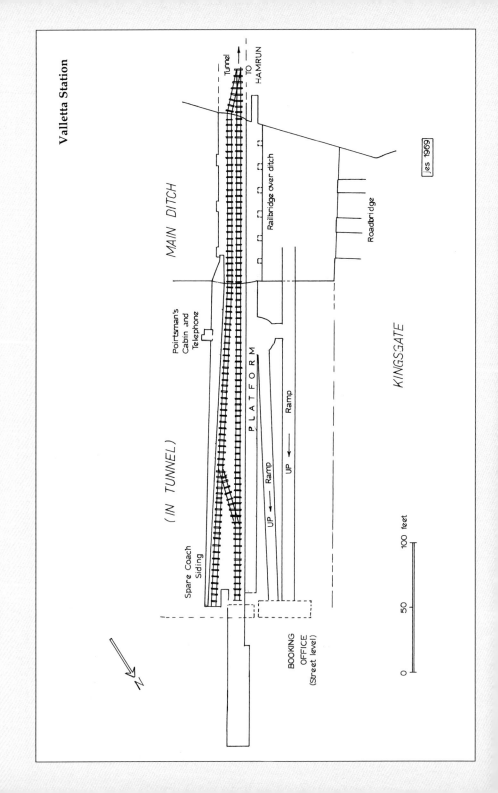

Valletta Station

MAIN DITCH

(IN TUNNEL)

Tunnel

TO HAMRUN

Pointsman's Cabin and Telephone

Spare Coach Siding

PLATFORM

Railbridge over ditch

Roadbridge

Ramp

UP →

Ramp

UP →

KINGSGATE

BOOKING OFFICE (Street level)

jes 1969

N

0   50   100 feet

Valletta station, from the shadows it is mid-morning, probably in the early 1920s. The train is bound for Museum.

A. Pisani

Above: The end of the terminus and tunnel entrance at Valletta in a sorry and abandoned state after closure.   *Colling Turner*

Right: The former entrance to Valletta station in 2004. Access is down the steps between the phone booth on the right, and the tourist office on the left. Part of the Doric styling of the station's architecture can be seen in this view.
        Major D. Murray-Bligh

surrounding edifices of the old Porta Reale and the Opera House. The elevation embraced nine columns supporting a roof framed with a stone pediment. There were entrances, giving access to the manager's room and booking offices on the left and right respectively of an entrance hall, and admitting passengers to the station by means of stairways. Dr Graham - and others - who travelled regularly on the line between 1896 and 1900 say that there were sloping ways or ramps enabling passengers to walk down to the platform. The alteration was probably carried out to ease the flow of passengers to and from the station as their numbers increased over the years. The platform was an ample one, being about 180 ft long with a depth of some 15 ft.

Immediately upon entering the station from the main ditch, the single line branched into two and there was a crossover at the terminus end, allowing engines to run-round their trains. There was a watering point. A few yards of spare track beyond the crossover at the end of the tunnel was often used as a siding for spare coaches, and barrels laid out along the track hereabouts were for the collection of dropped unburnt coal. Cinders were always sold.

The rear length of the platform was neatly railed off from the considerable drop to ground level of the viaduct. There were standard lamps at intervals along the railings. At platform level there was no name plate nor any other printed indication that the station was Valletta. Presumably everyone knew.

On leaving Valletta, to the accompaniment of the ringing of a handbell (as often in Victorian England) and the blowing of the guard's whistle, the train crossed the old ditch and plunged immediately through the ancient walls and on under Floriana in a tunnel rather less than 1,000 yards long south-westerly, a direction it was to maintain for about one mile. The tunnel, an unlined one cut through the solid rock, had three ventilating shafts, one emerging where Neptune now holds aquatic court, one flanking the edges of the Floriana granaries, and one between Floriana station and the end of the tunnel. These shafts, which were those used in the construction work, were later so re-designed as to make it impossible for anything to be thrown down on to the line. The article in *The Engineer* quoted above says of the tunnel that,

. . . the alignment was settled after much consideration, in order to meet, as far as possible, the requirements of the Military and Civil authorities, which was no easy matter, a tunnel directly through the outworks of an important fortress being almost unprecedented. It was subsequently discovered that an ancient subterranean reservoir - the position of which had not been previously known - would be intersected by the proposed line. In order to avoid this reservoir without altering the general alignment of the tunnel, it was decided to go round it, and so the tunnel has the rare feature of a double 'S' curve in the middle of it. The delicate operation of setting out this peculiar alignment underground was successfully accomplished by the resident engineer so that the headings met with a difference of about one inch only.

The deviation, of rather more than 150 yards, caused a screeching of train wheels which together with the smoke must - in spite of the ventilating shafts - have presented a grim vignette quite alien to the general Maltese scene.

Floriana station was in the tunnel here at a depth of 90 ft below ground and about 850 yards from Valletta station. It was, therefore, only some 150 yards

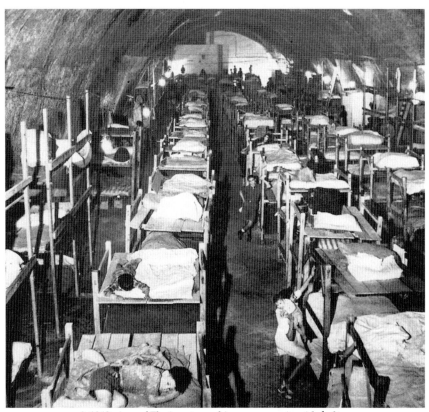

A 1943 view of Floriana tunnel in use as an air raid shelter.

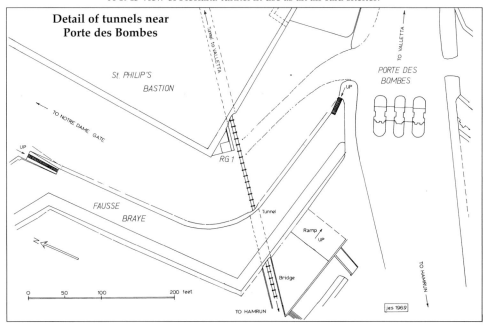

Detail of tunnels near Porte des Bombes

St. PHILIP'S BASTION

Turn to VALLETTA

TO VALLETTA

PORTE DES BOMBES

TO NOTRE DAME GATE

UP

UP

RG 1

FAUSSE BRAYE

UP

Tunnel

Ramp
UP

N

Bridge

0   50   100   200 feet

TO HAMRUN

TO HAMRUN

jes 1969

from the opposite end of the tunnel where it emerged from St Philip's Bastion. The station building, a simple entrance and booking hall, was at ground level above the tunnel, near to the Methodist church and the Argotti Gardens on the Marsamxett side. The many stairs necessary to reach the platform were so arranged as to make their use as easy as possible. Space for the platform was provided by increasing the span of arch forming the roof of the tunnel, on one side only.

Floriana, it seems, was never a popular station. Perhaps people were reluctant to penetrate the unattractive depths; or perhaps it was the economics of situation. Passengers were not likely to book from Floriana to Valletta. Such a trip in the dark would be irrelevant to the Maltese way of life, and those intending to travel in the direction of Notabile from Floriana probably found it equally if not more convenient to begin their journey at Valletta.

In the tunnel there was a falling gradient - towards Notabile - of 1 in 65. Thence to 3 miles 440 yards the gradients were generally level; and a continuous ascent began from 3 miles 440 yards to the end of the line. This was shown in succession as 1 in 66, increasing to 1 in 50 for the greater part of the distance developing into short bursts of 1 in 40 from Attard to Salvatore and on into Notabile station where there was a short level before a final similar climb through the tunnel to Museum. This tunnel was used in World War II as a major air-raid shelter, and now carries cables and water conduits.

The rails emerged at St Philip's Bastion, the portal, at a fairly acute angle with the carriageway, looking much in harmony with the towering bastion walls. As it began the crossing of the carriageway, the first of the 14 Railway Guard Huts RG1 (now a bar) was encountered. The catena, knowing of and doubtless hearing the approach of the train, connected his chains to the clasps on the stanchions, one chain on either side of the line, thus indicating to road users that they could not cross the line. Then he stood in the roadway at the side of the line and waved his white flag to indicate to the driver that the train could safely be taken across the road. Not all catenas would feel the need to exercise such vigilance as he at No. 1. One imagines that 13 and 14, out in the fields in the country approaching Notabile would have to deal mostly with goats and the odd farm cart, and from their huts in the bright noonday sun or the long purple shadows of evening could see the train from afar, coming from either direction. These guard huts were austere buildings, purely functional and megalithic in concept. Today Nos. 6, 11 and 12 also remain, but unused.

Having then emerged from St Philip's Bastion and crossed the carriageway the railway had by no means cleared the formidable old fortifications. It now entered another tunnel some 33 yards long, penetrating an outer bastion, the Fausse Braye, and emerging from this outer bastion wall - again with the portal at an angle to the line - crossed the last and outer ditch by a charming little six-arched bridge (still extant) built to harmonise with the general surroundings, including buttressed side walls. After this there was a final short cutting through the outer walls.

Now the railway entered a strangely neglected and wild piece of country, lower than the city bastions and therefore raising the line on to an embankment. On the right there were two large cemeteries and on the left more of the city

Entrance to tunnel at Porte des Bombes in 1967.   *Cyril Smith*

The viaduct from the short tunnel to the cutting at Porte des Bombes in 1967.   *Cyril Smith*

Tunnel entrance on Museum side at Porte des Bombes in 1967.   *Colling Turner*

High summer, with staff in summer uniform. A train from Museum has just arrived at Hamrun in the 1920s.

walls - the St Francis Ravelin and the continuation of the Fausse Braye and the bastion wall. This ragged terrain extended for only some 60 or 70 yards before the railway crossed the Princess Melita Road. There was first a stone arch over the tree-lined pavement, a girder bridge over the road itself and then several more stone arches as the bridge progressed further over a lane connecting with the Princess Melita Road and so to a pleasant straight run almost parallel with the Blata il Baida Road on the left. One or two small tracked roads hereabouts, for example to the Jewish cemetery and to a small holding, did not appear to have any protection; the line just went straight across them.

A postcard of the early 1900s, poor copies of which still circulate in Malta, shows a train on the Princess Melita Road bridge. It looks surprisingly large on the bridge which therefore was obviously smaller than one imagines it to have been. In the foreground is a herd of milking goats with their goatherds.

We left the train running along beside the Blata il Baida Road. At about one mile from Valletta the line swung from south-west to west and RG2 stood here, where a small road from Strada Reale (the continuation of Blata il Baida) gave access to the Mile End sports ground. It has been said by some drivers that an exciting football match at the sports ground brought trains to a halt for a short time. The halts could not have been lengthy ones because there was not much timetable leeway and the railway did not have a reputation for unpunctuality.

For a distance now of perhaps 800 yards before reaching Hamrun station at 1 mile 635 yards, the track passed along the backs of houses in the Marsa-Hamrun complex with much the same atmosphere of domestic proximity as in many a local English line. RG3 was at the beginning of this now westerly 800 yard run, where a country road struck out from Strada Reale over the fields towards Msida. J.E. Swann in *The Times of Malta* wrote of this section that the 'run into the adjacent station (i.e. Hamrun) afforded an intimate view of the life of the residents on to their backyards and rear windows'. In this area over the now almost vanished tiny fields of the urban farmers and past the already encroaching suburbs the line tended to be embanked and to encompass a series of beautifully built and conceived curves. As we shall see, by the time the suburbs had been left behind from, say, the level crossing just outside Attard station the character of the route changed as it entered real countryside and faced the remainder of its steepest climbs.

To return to the embankments and Hamrun station. As with all building in Malta, whatever the nature, loving craftsmanship and patient skill are fundamental features. None of the embankments in this central section of the line were very high, the vertical central axes probably varying between eight and 16 feet. The embankment sides were invariably stone-lined, the mason-work being expertly carried out in the dry-stone fashion. Guard rails were furnished at certain points. Today flowers flourish on and around them, and the caper plant fastens into the thousands of niches. In winter the little narcissi and the gay oxalia flourish, followed by the flowers of the 'tumultuous spring', the horn of plenty, campion, poppy, snapdragon, lady's finger and wild-thyme all to the accompaniment of yellow-dominating clouds of cape sorrel. *The Engineer* for 13th April, 1883, says of the embankment that

A 1960s view of the bridge at the end of the embankment near Hamrun in 1967. *Colling Turner*

The building in the centre in this 1967 view of Hamrun contained a drawing room, dining room and apprentices room. It was demolished in 1968. The building to the left was part of the Technical School and was not built until after closure of the railway.

. . . land being very valuable and reluctantly parted with, advantage has been taken of the circumstance that the cuttings are almost entirely in rock to form the embankment with hand-packed pitched slopes of ½ to 1, the more regularly shaped stones being selected for the outside, and the interior of the bank filled up with rubble. The train consequently presents the curious appearance of running along the top of a wall.

Hamrun was the engineering headquarters. It was a busy complex of tree-lined large station with surrounding workshops. There were two platforms and the canopied building containing waiting rooms, ticket and luggage offices was on the southern platform. All station buildings from Hamrun onwards to the Museum terminus had certain common aspects. They were substantial, had some style and were in proportion to their ancillary surroundings. The black lettering announcing the name of the station or offices was large, plain in good style and common to them all. The naming was not carried out in the English way of erecting boards at each end of the station parallel to the platform, nor in the continental manner high up on the side of the building and at right-angles to the line. The practice on the Malta Railway was to name stations over exit doorways; in a straight line where door-frames were straight (as at Attard) or in a semi-circle if top door frames were curved (as at Museum). There were also seats and lamps in the English tradition. The language used was English apart of course from the actual place names. The earliest timetables were in Italian. A picture postcard of Attard station, printed in Italy, refers to it as 'Altaro Railway Station'. Later timetables were in English and indeed English in style and layout.

Hamrun northern platform snuggled into a background of trees. Lines led off from the main line to the sheds and workshops. Today the scene at the site is very different; the trees have gone and in their places are mundane commercial buildings. However it is a pleasant surprise to peer through some large gates near the Technical School and see the station buildings standing in very good order in a yard, giving the appearance of having been bodily transplanted from elsewhere. There was a double track in the station with the usual crossover facilities. As the line left Hamrun station for Museum a semaphore signal could be seen just clear of the station buildings, on the platform, and rising to some 20 ft in height. The signal was evidently considered to be a necessary addition to the general telephone control system. Its function was probably that of synchronising local control of locomotives and rolling stock and on and off shed and shops, with the general running of the line. The semaphore arm was painted green with a vertical white stripe near the end of the arm. It was worked by hand-winch, wheel and rope, the arm swinging downwards from the horizontal. In the horizontal, the signal was one of CAUTION; and completely down, hanging vertically, the signal was to PROCEED. The arm pointed trackwards.

The telephone system of general control consisted in a series of bells whereby the departure of a train from one station to another was notified to all concerned by an appropriate number of beats on the bell, each station having a definite number of beats assigned to it. This system coupled with the timetabling and the average speeds enabled staff to ensure control over movement to such an

The embankment west of Hamrun, looking towards Valletta in 1967.   *Cyril Smith*

An under bridge under Msida embankment in 1967.

extent that, although many millions of passengers were carried during the lifetime of the railway, there was no serious accident.

Passing the signal, and on towards Museum, the line turned on a sharp curve to hold a course rather west of north for a little under half a mile. As it approached Msida station the track was raised on to an embankment some 300 yds long. At the beginning of this embankment there was a small bridge designed to give a farmer access to his fields, and close by Msida station there was a bridge giving access to a (then) solitary house in Tal Fatati.

Msida station was entered at 1 mile 1,345 yards. The platform was never more than a baked-earth raised portion with boundary flagstones. It seems this little place from the very beginning fulfilled the functions of a halt as implied by that word in English railway practice.

Stations - with the exception of the more important ones - tended to drop in and out of timetables or never to be mentioned at all. One - Santa Venera - is said by some sources to have existed and to be denied this privilege by others. It may well be that there was a location on the line convenient and near to Santa Venera which by custom became a recognised stopping place. There are varying reports as to whether or not trains were in the habit of stopping anywhere on the line when signalled to do so by intending passengers.

If we include Santa Venera, 12 stations may be listed in sequence: Valletta, Floriana, Hamrun, Msida, Santa Venera, Birkirkara, Balzan, San Antonio, Attard, San Salvatore, Notabile and Museum. The timetable at the opening of the railway quoted Valletta, Hamrun, Msida, Birkirkara, San Antonio, Attard, San Salvatore and Notabile. The Manager's report for 1910 says there were six stations but does not name them. By 1924 timetables were quoting Valletta, Hamrun, Birkirkara, Attard and Museum, with San Salvatore and Balzan in footnotes. At this time, however, the remaining stations - with the exception of Floriana and the possible exception of Santa Venera - still existed, so it may be presumed they were being much used as 'Halts'.

The historical development was that the railway finally possessed six major stations, Valletta, Hamrun, Birkirkara, Attard, Notabile and Museum and four minor stations or halts, Msida, Balzan, San Antonio and San Salvatore. Santa Venera was a possible fifth in the minor class and Floriana closed in 1900. In later years, at least, it seems that trains did not stop at halts unless there were passengers or goods parcels to set down or pick up.

If one was waiting at a halt one signalled the train to stop: if travelling, the guard arranged the required stop. One timetable says: 'with the exception of the 4.30, 5.20 and 6 am and the 5.10 and 5.30 pm all other trains will stop at any intermediate station at the request of the passengers'. The timetable also assumed the reader to have considerable local knowledge. One such document for instance refers to Notabile (Museum) station and says in a footnote that the 5.20 am would start from Notabile and not from Museum station. Local workmen obviously understood what was meant. In fact workmen's trains never used the Museum station. Valletta to Notabile was the total extent of their use and these trains were shunted at Notabile for return journeys to Valletta.

On leaving Msida the permanent way returned to its general westerly direction for rather more than two more miles, that is to the end of the cutting

Birkirkara Station

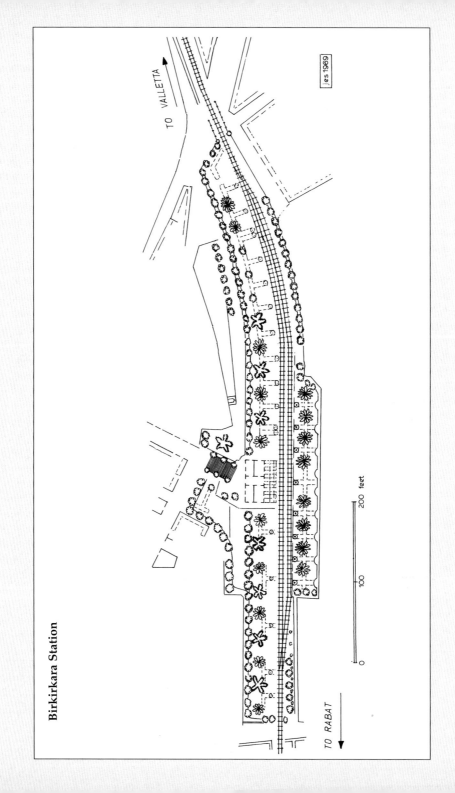

TO VALLETTA

jes 1969

TO RABAT

200 feet

100

0

beyond Attard station. After crossing a minor road immediately upon leaving Msida a further hundred yards saw a level crossing across an important suburban road between Hamrun and Msida with RG4 on the right of the line. Now it was open countryside at field level with clear views and a straight run. This was one of the fastest sections of the railway. In 400 yards from RG4 a country road coming right across from Qormi via Santa Venera to Msida crossed the line. RG5 was here, again like RG4 on the right-hand side. If the halt at Santa Venera existed - whether or not officially - it must have been here at the level crossing on the opposite side from the guard hut. Some 350 yards of almost straight run brought a crossing over a road used by farmers to and from Santa Venera and the fields. RG6 at this point was on the left of the line.

On reaching the outskirts of Birkirkara the route returned to ground level, passed across a country lane with RG7 on the right in the Fleur-de-Lys suburb of the town, again seeing the backs of houses in the Psaila Street area and so across the Fleur-de-Lys road - a wide crossing requiring careful control by station staff - and into Birkirkara station at approximately 2 miles 1,658 yards. Unlike most of the other stations on the line, Birkirkara and Attard not only had spaciousness at their disposal, but also attractive and extensive backgrounds. Indeed both came to occupy by chance and by subsequent development what may be described as natural little park sites. Birkirkara station was in a setting on the southern boundary of the town between two main roads coming into the town at right angles to the station.

There was a small town square on the right on passing across the Fleur-de-Lys road and an imposing gateway entrance to the station enclave. A church dominating the background completed the scene. The two platforms faced each other across double track through the station. The southern (down) platform was built out from an old wall and a most decorative effect was achieved by a series of circular flower beds on the platform and ramblers trailed round the buttresses of the wall. There were seats in the shelter of the wall and more flowers on shelving at shoulder-height. The northern (up) platform housed the station buildings, a dignified two-storey structure with side balconies, and stone-columned roof railing and a substantial sun-canopy extending out over the platform. Distributed along the platform on either side of the canopy were four lamp-posts, English Victorian in every detail, down to fluting and ladder arm-supports. They had oil lamps in their lanterns. The station name was painted above the doorway, in the general style already described. There was a path across the tracks from platform to platform.

Birkirkara station was a place to go to, not invariably in order to catch a train, but also to sit, chat or snooze and watch the traffic go by, in much the same way as is done in some airports today. That enterprising and imaginative manager Nicholas Buhagiar had been quick to observe these scenic possibilities and to develop them. In addition to the decorative palms and spring and summer flowers already mentioned he also grew orange and lemon trees. In 1912 he produced a number of very large urns for flowers, some of which can be seen at Hamrun and Birkirkara today. Mr Buhagiar realised that he was in a position to create a series of gardens in an otherwise somewhat tree-less austere landscape. He was quite happy to have people sitting in his upland stations admiring the

Birkirkara station after the turn of the century with a train bound for Valletta.

R. Ellis

20 · Railway Station (Birchircara).

A postcard view of Birkirkara station showing the beautifully cared for horticulture, looking along the gently curving platform towards Museum.   *John Alsop Collection*

One of the Manning, Wardle 0-6-0Ts arrives at Birkirkara station from Valletta.
                    John Alsop Collection

Birchircara Railway Station, Malta.

A 1967 view of Birkirkara station in use as offices after the railway's closure.   *Colling Turner*

Birkirkara station looks in fine condition in this 2004 view.   *Major D. Murray-Bligh*

greenery. It was not terribly important that they purchase a ticket. It *was* important that they appreciated the existence of the line.

He achieved these results, says one writer,

> . . . in a dry land by an ingenious system for utilising rain water drained from the tracks and adjacent highways. Pits, from five to six feet deep, are dug in the subsoil close to the tracks at the stations, and are lined with rubble walls. A system of horizontal trenches of similar depth and filled with stone chippings is led from the pits to irrigate as large an area as is desired, and in this way the subsoil above the porous rock and the rock itself is always kept in a moist condition, as loss by evaporation is thereby avoided. In practice, the pits are constructed beneath the platforms, inlets being provided in the platform faces at ground level.

At Birkirkara station there was a water tank for re-fuelling locomotives.

With the closure of the line Birkirkara station buildings were brought into use as Government offices. A photograph taken during this period shows a sharp and sad decline from the luxuriant and well-planned platform gardens of the railway period. Every vestige of the garden has disappeared to be replaced by earthen pathways. Now, however, in 2004, we see the site has been sympathetically restored to something akin to its former beauty.

The railway left Birkirkara enclave in a similar way to its entrance, by passing through boundary walls. It ran somewhat south of the western suburbs of the town. However RG8 on the right and RG9 on the left (Strada Imriehel) were passed in rapid succession in the network of small outer streets, followed by a straight run almost due west into Balzan station at 3 miles 570 yards. The little halt consisted of one stone-bound earth platform and RG10 combined, on a narrow country road connecting two east-west roads, Strada Reale and Strada Sant'Antonio. After leaving Balzan there was a swing to south-west into San Antonio station, at 3 miles 900 yards, a halt again situated on a lane connecting

The trackbed and stone embankment at San Anton in 1967.   *Cyril Smith*

The bridge over the Attard-Birkirkara road, about 150 yards from Attard station, looking towards Valletta. The train is bound for Museum. *A. Pisani*

San Anton in post-World War II years, with the aqueduct visible in the background. This view looks towards Attard. Attard church can be seen in the distance. *Cyril Smith*

the two east-west lateral roads already mentioned. This station had in its earlier days a liberal background of palm, carob and tamarisk trees and a certain festive air. It was mostly used by visitors to the Gardens of the San Anton Palace. There was a crossing loop.

After Balzan the route swung back to its western axis and began the approach to Attard station. It was now running on an embankment whose sides were rather steeper than those in the Hamrun and Msida sections. The passage over the Attard-Birkirkara road was by means of a stout girder bridge with stone side buttresses. There followed the final climb into Attard station at 3 miles 1,400 yards.

Attard, one felt, was the first of the uplands stations. The word uplands, in addition to its normal meaning is used to emphasise that here was the dividing line between two types of terrain served by the railway. The economic functions of the towns surrounding Valletta had expanded rapidly during the lifetime of the railway. Indeed this development continues today. The old parishes of Birkirkara and Lija are being devoured by the hungry new township of Hamrun forming thus a large and complex urbanisation. This process may well reach Mdina in time, but for the moment at any rate and from the point of view of the little railway, Attard station was a recognisable dividing point. One could stand on either platform and look back towards Valletta, below the fields to Hamrun and beyond to the capital; and appreciate how much the train had climbed since leaving Valletta.

Attard Station

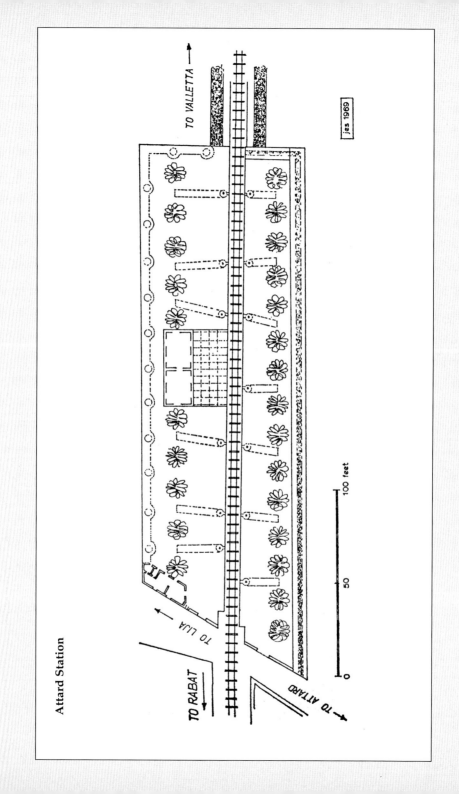

TO RABAT

TO LIJA

TO ATTARD

TO VALLETTA →

jes 1969

0   50   100 feet

Attard station showing the method used by the railway in naming over the station doors.

R. Ellis

A splendid photograph of Attard station in high summer *circa* 1910. The train has just arrived from Museum.   *John Alsop Collection*

The site of Attard station in a state of decay in 1967.   *Cyril Smith*

Like Birkirkara, Attard was spacious, with deep platforms upon which in spring a light breeze was always playing and where in summer the heat beat down fiercely. The light seemed all day to be intense. Again there were circular flower beds on the northern (up) platform with a palm in the centre of each bed. The station building on the up platform was an unpretentious rectangular block, with canopy, the usual offices and the name Attard over the main doorway. There were also a number of lamp posts along the platforms as at Birkirkara. Entrance was actually from the main road to the immediate west and there were booking facilities at this strategic point. This way of entrance to the station meant that the platforms assumed in a sense more importance than the main building.

I recall seeing in the 1960s, on the site of Attard station, a stout iron noticeboard, somewhat in the style of those formidable iron boards once to be found on British railways giving warnings of the consequences of trespassing. The notice read, 'These carob trees grown from seed at Taxbriex Villa nursery in 1895 were transplanted in this station (Attard) in 1897' (*see photograph on page 115*).

Attard did not have double track in the station precincts although it was sufficiently important for this and had the available space for such construction. Timetables as late as the early 1920s show that in spite of this track arrangement Attard was a terminating and starting point for some trains (workmen's 8.04 am arrival, 8.06 am departure).

On leaving Attard the train was seen across the important Strada St Antonio by station staff and immediately entered a substantially-constructed cutting some 700 yards long and petering off in a further 100 yards. The route was straight for about the first 600 yards of this cutting but after RG11 it swung south-west in the direction of San Salvatore. This south-westerly 'dog-leg' was about 1 mile 350 yards long, reaching to a point just beyond the Zebbug road.

The cutting did not pierce any land on either side much higher than its own walls. It was a right-angled construction whose sides were quite often the natural rock either topped off with drystone walling or totally wall-patched. As it ran down again to field level approaching San Salvatore, complete walling could be seen, masonry in the lower brickwork and loose walling in the higher. At its deepest it was perhaps 12 ft to 14 ft. At intervals in the rock face there were refuges in the shape of small cave-like apertures with entrance steps. Presumably these were for the use of local farmers or anyone careless enough to be caught walking along the cutting when a train entered it. One feels these refuges might have been well used because, for example, in 1912 there were some 14 trains making the full length journey every day excepting Sundays.

Some 300 yards into the cutting the line passed under a track which linked Attard with the Tal-Mirakli road. The bridge was a stone single-arch whose supports were built into each side of the cutting, still in position today. Looking up the cutting from Attard, with the bridge framing the distant scene is to evoke one of the most striking memories of the line; one that serves to emphasise the unique combination of rocky Mediterranean landscape and little locomotives and rolling stock built in green England.

In rather less than half a mile from Attard station the railway ran across the Ta Kali road, a secondary route linking Attard with Notabile and with several

Road bridge over the stone-lined cutting about ½ mile from Attard station in 1967.

Colling Turner

Site of San Salvatore station looking towards Museum in 1967.   *Colling Turner*

lanes and villages. RG11 (still standing) was located here on the Notabile side of the road. Continuing on its way, with the cutting gradually dying away, the line, as has been said, now went generally south-west in gentle curves to a point just beyond the Zebbug road. In this open farmland between RG11 and San Salvatore station the track ran along on a small embankment, a prominent isolated feature of this particular landscape, to run into San Salvatore, a station of halt status, at 4 miles 1,200 yards.

San Salvatore was a spacious, sunlit place beneath the palms and carobs. There was a platform with one small station building and very little of the attention to floral detail (except for the planting of palm trees) as seen at Attard and Birkirkara, an indication of its relegation - even if unconsciously - to the status of halt. There was a crossing loop here adjacent to a small viaduct of four arches across a wied.* In the later years of the railway this loop fell into disuse, but in earlier days it was used when extra trains were laid on for the festival of St Paul, San Salvatore being a favourite and nearby country spot for town-dwellers in holiday festive mood. In sad contrast also, the halt was used by patients, staff and visitors connected with a mental hospital just east of the station, marked on all contemporary maps, 'Lunatic Asylum'.

Leaving San Salvatore the line passed under the Attard-Mdina road, the Via Notabile, and entered the upland fields on the last open stage of its journey to Museum. The bridge under was really a small tunnel some 25 yards long. The angle between railway track and main road was an acute one and in consequence the inner lining of the little tunnel was carried out in a series of transversal flutings (*see overleaf*).

Now the gradients became even heavier as the railway progressed across the fields sometimes open on either side and sometimes between dry-stone walls. At about 700 yards from San Salvatore station the route crossed a quiet country lane and RG12 (still standing), then in another 300 yards the Ta Srina Lane and RG13 to be followed by a straight run of 400 yards to RG14 guarding the Zebbug-Mdina road. These last three guard-huts could not have seen much more in the way of road traffic than farmers with their carts and the occasional herd of goats.

So for nearly 50 years one of the main features of the scene across these few miles from San Salvatore to Mdina was the full-throated sound of the little engines as they climbed towards the terminus, and from the ancient city walls the view nearly always included a vertical plume of smoke, the glint of brass caught in the sun and a caterpillar of four-wheeled coaches.

About 250 yards beyond RG14 the line took a long gentle curve to swing almost due west and straight for about 650 yards. This total section across the open cultivated fields and at the same level can today be recognised, in part at least, as a very useful country lane. Only its carefully designed flow and alignment serves to distinguish it from the normal haphazard meandering country route.

On the completion of this section there was a swing to the final alignment, north-west and in a straight line only slightly 'kinked' at Notabile station for the remaining 1,880 yards. Just at the turn the line crossed a bridge over what must have been one of the longest and most wandering of the internal country roads

* A small valley.

The bridge under the Attard-Mdina road (Via Notabile), long since demolished. The road here is now of course flat and the casual observer would imagine that the line terminated in the adjacent San Salvatore station. This rare view was probably taken shortly after the line's closure.

A. Pisani and N. Azzopardi

in the island. Running north and south it served only scattered farms, with feeders to Notabile and Rabat on its western flank.

Now the railway, although of course still climbing, began to leave field-level and to cut between stone walls on either side. Finally this became a deep and leafy cutting surmounted by iron railings enclosing fields of clover running beside Strada Corsa and into Notabile (Rabat) station at 6 miles 600 yards. The run over the fields from San Salvatore to Notabile was the longest on the line between stations.

It may be confusing that we name this station as Notabile when our map of the line names it Rabat. Mr A.R. Bennett in his article written in 1927 to which we have already made reference writes as follows,

The years have endowed Notabile with an unusual collection of names. The Arabs during their occupation (AD870-1090) called it Mdina, but such a heathen cognomen grieved the soul of good King Alphonso of Aragon, so, when he had turned them out, he decreed that henceforth it should be known as Notabile. But even Kings of Aragon could not always have things their own way and, as time went on, the Italians christened it Citta Vecchia (the old city); and a suburb Rabato, greater in extent and population than itself, grew up in immediate proximity. So it has come to pass that would-be passengers for the venerable fortress, within the walls of which St Paul converted Publius, the ruler of Malta in those days - afterwards St Publio - to Christianity, may ask for tickets to Medina, Notabile, Citta Vecchia, or Rabato whichever rises to the tongue first, and yet he landed at one and the same platform. And so a guard or porter will inform you on enquiry that the train will be sure to stop at any and all of those places.

Robin Bryans, in his book *Malta* published in 1966, writes,

Rabat, with its winding streets, squares lined with evergreen oaks and pepper trees, its Baroque churches and Roman remains and early Christian catacombs, was, in spite of so many important features, a suburb of Mdina, from the foot of whose walls it extended along the ridge. The name Rabat conjured up North Africa, where Rabat meant 'the environs inside the city wall' - which exactly described Malta's Rabat. Also, Mdina is the Arabic medina, 'the city' - which again Malta's Medina was, a walled city . . . What had been the Roman city of Melita became the Medina when the Arabs conquered Malta in 870. They enclosed the end spur of the city's ridge by building a great wall and a ditch.

There are many Medinas in the Eastern World; one recalls the Old Medina in *Casablanca* to give a single, in this case romantic, example.

Thus we see the ancient Maltese town standing on the only prominent physical feature on the Island with its lowland suburb of Rabat eventually growing larger than its parent. Rabat station was where one alighted for the old city above. The station consisted of little more than one platform, simply because there was no need for anything more elaborate. It dealt largely with workers of many sorts, travelling to their livelihoods in both places from their homes in the Valletta conurbation. If the work was in the old city you climbed the upward stairway and entered through the magnificent gate-bridge. That inveterate walker Coleridge who had visited and fallen in love with the Island many years before the birth of the railway, would have loved it. Byron, who deigned to call in, would possibly have not been so enthusiastic. The reader will

Railway guard hut No. 12 (*see map on page 8*) on a country road between Attard and Museum.

A postcard view of Notabile station.   *John Alsop Collection*

probably have noted my indiscriminate use of Rabat and Notabile; so too was the case when the railway was running.

It is the case that in one sense Notabile was the end of the line from the purely local commercial point of view.

The cutting had not always been sylvan. Photographs taken on the opening day show the bare earth sides of the embankment, the complete absence of vegetation and the station building standing prominently in its stark surroundings. There was only one platform, a loop coming off the main line to serve it and rejoining beyond the northern end of the platform. The station was of course below the level of the road. A lane, with steps, led down to it. Later a building similar to that on the platform, and at roadside level, was added. This building although in the style peculiar to the railway gave the place something of the air of an English country station.

Again, in true English country tradition, the journey from Notabile station to town was longish and difficult. Getting up to the old city and its suburb of Rabat from the station was described by one writer (Crotchet, in *Times of Malta*, 1963) as follows:

> The trains used to stop at a station placed at the bottom of a wide cutting 100 feet or so below the level of that suburb (i.e. Rabat). Leaving the train, passengers went up an incline (or rather, a steep flight of stairs) to attain the Siggiewi-Rabat road, along which they then had to toil up the steep rough hill that served, and serves, as the finish of the Mnarja horse races which left them footsore and winded with yet further gradients to negotiate. After his experience with our 'cursed streets of stairs' Byron would surely have fallen out with his muse had the train been there for him to patronise during that unfortunate visit to Malta.

Within a few yards of leaving Notabile station the line entered its fourth and final tunnel. This was a major engineering and constructional achievement. It pierced the hill on which stands the old capital of Mdina. Some 770 yards long, it ran through belts of blue clay and upper coralline limestone. There were eight square-sectional ventilating shafts distributed along its length. Both the Notabile and Museum portals and supporting walls were imposing pieces of architecture, the latter (still intact) carrying the date of construction over the arch keystone. The tunnel emerged from the defence walls of the Mdina fortress almost immediately beneath the Roman Museum. About 100 yards from the exit the railway entered Museum (also known as Imtarfa/Mtarfa) station at 6 miles 1,600 yards. The station stood in open country on a shelf between Mdina Hill and the valley of the Wied il March at right angles beyond. On a hill on the opposite side of the valley was the Imtarfa military barracks.

From the area linking Rabat with Notabile a specially constructed tree-lined road led down to the station, at first parallel to the line and then when opposite the station turning at right angles to lead into it. Arrived there, the road widened and in front of the entrance, in the middle of the road, there was another of Mr Buhagiar's favourite circular flower beds. The station building was a solid affair with a substantial canopy. Windows and doors had curved portals and the words 'Museum Station' were painted around the arched portal of the central doorway whence also a very stylish lamp was suspended. There

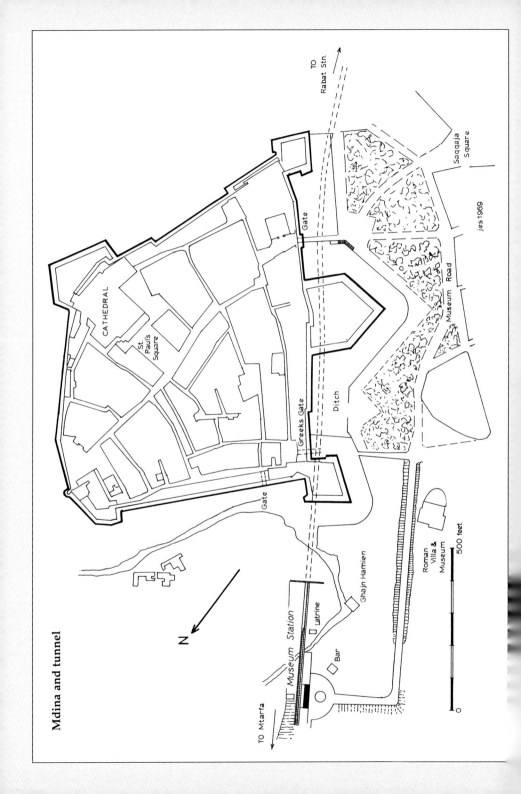

Mdina and tunnel

Museum station and terminus of line beyond. This view is taken from Mdina city walls. An example of the outstanding work of the Ellis family.   *R. Ellis*

Railway staff pose with the engine as it waits to leave Museum with a train for Valletta. The inspection pit can be seen on the left.　　　*John Alsop Collection*

The tunnel mouth viewed from Museum station in the 1950s. The tunnel was at one time used
for growing mushrooms.   *Colling Turner*

Museum station. The park-like approach to the station was designed by Mr Buhagiar. The military barracks can be seen in the distance.

The station approach at Museum some 20-odd years after closure.   *Colling Turner*

were no standard lamps on the platform, as at other stations. The lettering 'First Class' and the like was painted horizontally on the standards beneath the fan-windows and there were the usual platform seats.

A loop line enabled the engine to run-round its train and on the platform line just past the loop there was an inspection pit. The line ran on some 400 yards beyond the station, alongside the road to an abrupt terminus rather astonishingly against a brick wall surrounding a building at 7 miles 240 yards. This length was suitable for stock storage requirements but whether it was ever extensively used for this purpose is doubtful. It was more likely a part of a scheme to reach as far as Imtarfa Barracks, but if so it fell short of this aim by a stiff hill climb. The extension to Museum was in any case carried out at the wish of the military, although it is as well to bear in mind the original grandiose 19th century plan to cover the island with a railway network. Nicholas Buhagiar knew of this plan and undoubtedly he always hoped to see some or all of it carried out. Only in his later years as Manager would he come to appreciate that it was impossible of achievement and turn his energies in many other directions.

It has been said also that in the early days there was Maltese opposition to the line because it was considered to be a part of military ambitions. But if there ever was much opposition it was certainly not sustained. During World War I the railway ran many troop trains non-stop to Museum from Valletta. These trains had the longest rakes in the history of the line and doubtless they - and possibly others! - ran right on as far as the brickwall end of the line.

These last few hundred yards beyond Museum also involved some considerable civil engineering works. The crossing of the little valley was made upon a substantial viaduct with a noble single-arch stone bridge in the centre of the valley, all still standing.

Museum station in 1964.   *A. Pisani*

Museum viaduct viewed from the north.

Museum viaduct and the end of the line.   *Colling Turner*

Chapter Three

The Running of the Railway

We have seen that as a private company the railway failed to pay its way and furthermore the failure was a rapid one after a most promising start.

The Engineer for 13th April, 1883, was one of several authorities which considered the line to have a most promising life ahead of it.

Casual visitors to Malta [it said] are apt to come away with the impression that the island is a mere rocky and barren appendage to the great harbours and naval and military establishments, of which Valletta is the nucleus, and surprise has even been expressed that railways should be wanted in the island at all. As a fact, however, much of the soil of Malta is extremely fertile, and the density of the population is quite exceptional, as will be seen from the following comparative table:

	Isle of Wight	Isle of Man	Malta
Area in square miles	164	227	95
Population	56,000	55,000	*133,000
Population per square mile	341	242	1,400
Miles of railway constructed	34 ¼	43 ½	6 ¾
Population per mile of railway	1,600	1,264	21,000

* Today more than 330,000 (nearly 3,500 per square mile)

P.P. Castagna estimated the takings at the beginning to be of the order of £50 to £60 a day, dropping during the lifetime of the company to about £13 a day, and he considered the company to have lost about £80,000. He did not give his views on the reasons for this decline. Of course the significance of takings per day - whether they are good or bad - can only be assessed when several other factors are considered. Similar figures for later years were as follows:

	Gross Revenue	No. of Passengers
1902-1903	£9,020, i.e. approximately £25 per day*	924,350
1903-1904	£9,272, i.e. approximately £26 per day*	959,130
1907-1908	£8,419, i.e. approximately £24 per day*	914,903
1910-1911	£6,507, i.e. approximately £18 per day*	742,936
1929-1930	£7,092, i.e. approximately £19 per day*	681,200
1930-1931	£4,706, i.e. approximately £13 per day*	497,297

* Working on a rounded figure of 360 days to the year.

In his article in *The Locomotive* for 15th September, 1927, A.R. Bennett says,

. . . about two millions of passengers are carried annually . . . coaches accommodating from 24 to 28 persons, but as passengers are allowed to stand on the platforms which have even seats for two or three and also straphang in the carriages, the carrying capacity is often demonstrably greatly in excess of the seating.

Beyer, Peacock 2-6-4T No. 7 at Museum station in 1918.

Nevertheless the carrying capacity would have had to be very much greater than seating capacity to manage two millions per year. The figure for 1929-30 was 681,200. That for 1927 is not available but is unlikely to have been so much greater than 1929-30. From official figures available the highest was 1903-4 when 959,130 were carried. The line would possibly have carried two millions per annum if there had been a demand for this. Rakes could have been lengthened as there would have been no serious platform difficulties. Nor could there have been staff or control problems. More motive power would have been required. But all this is academic.

In 1893, the first year of the Government running of the railway, the number of passengers carried was 630,000.

Passengers were by far the greatest single source of revenue and the standard fares of 1*d*. per mile first class and ½*d*. per mile second class, with a special rate for workmen of 2*d*. from Valletta to Notabile and concession rates for several classes and professions, apparently remained unchanged over the years. This would indicate (especially when one includes the workmen's fares) that Government looked upon the line as an essential component in the economic development of Malta. Thus it was prepared to support the continued existence of the railway. Much later, when motor transport emerged and was found to be cheaper than the railway, the story became a very different one.

It was this policy which decided the Government of Malta to reserve the right to acquire the line from the private company under the conditions mentioned above. The main reason was to ensure continuance of the service.

It emerges that one cannot exactly equate the running of the line under private ownership with that under Government, in the purely financial sense.

What, therefore, was the reason for the failure of the private company in such a comparatively short time? It may be that a timetable of seven trains a day each way excepting Sundays with at first three locomotives (and later four) to hand was too ambitious with the limited maintenance facilities then available; but it is more likely that there was a series of happenings contributing to the losses. A mechanical breakdown which occurred in Floriana tunnel during this critical period is a significant pointer. The incident must have done considerable harm to the company. Passengers on the train were probably both frightened and disgusted and the story of the breakdown doubtless spread rapidly over the island. There were many other such inconveniences and at the same time a steady decline in gross takings.

The purchase of a further locomotive - No. 4 - at a cost of more than £1,000 shortly before the end of the company's life shows that the then existing stud of three was too small. Further, according to Castagna, the first three locomotives were in such a poor state by 1889-90 that they had to be sent to the dockyard for repairs, involving the company in a bill of £4,000.

The Engineer for 13th April, 1883, reports that the '. . . central depot is at Hamrun, where engine and carriage sheds are provided'. There is no mention of workshops, hence the recourse to the dockyards.

So the losses mounted; and as further capital was not forthcoming and the maintenance facilities within the company were so limited, the end was inevitable. The line was closed on 1st April, 1890, and re-opened under Government control on 25th February, 1892. Government began by clearing the dockyard debt of £4,000.

One of the Manning, Wardle 0-6-0Ts is in the process of running round its train at Museum. It is high summer and the soldiers are in 'walking-out dress'. It may therefore be a party having a day out (R&R) and using the railway as the best and cheapest way of getting around.

John Alsop Collection

After the take-over had been completed, the following sums were voted:

For the purchase of new locomotives and ancillary equipment	£8,000
For employees salaries	£1,550
For coal, oil, telephones, gas, uniforms and tools	£2,780
Total	£12,330

This sum was eventually increased first to £16,000 and then to £19,000.

During the period of closure of slightly less than two years a considerable amount of works on permanent way, bridges and buildings was carried out and two locomotives (£4,060) and 17 carriages (£1,040) were purchased. In all the Malta Railway in its final form was worth at least £100,000.

Considerable sums were spent on renewal and maintenance of permanent way (in 1929-30 and 1930-31, the last two years, the sums respectively of £1,334 and £1,129 were spent). A railway some seven miles in length and with a lifetime of almost 50 years, must have had several thousands of pounds spent upon its permanent way. A partial explanation of the apparently heavy amounts spent in the earlier years, may lie in the recurring statement 'renewal of track'. With the increases in weight of locomotives and rolling stock and also with the increasing workings, it became apparent that the original track was not sufficiently strong and heavy. This original permanent way was of Vignoles steel rail weighing 45 lb. to the yard, fish-jointed, secured to the sleepers at the ends and middle of each rail by fang bolts, and at intermediate sleepers by dog spikes. The fang bolts had their units on the top of the flange of the rail so as to avoid opening out the road for screwing up. The dog spikes were cylindrical. The rail flanges were not notched, but the square washers of the fang bolts were placed chock up against the ends of the fish plates, so as to prevent the rails 'creeping' down the inclines. The oak sleepers were imported from Tunis. The later weight of line was 60 lb. to the yard, the rail being spiked directly to their sleepers.

In 1904 £604 was expended in 'reconstructing a portion of the line with heavier rails', the 1908 report mentions that 'new and heavier rails' were laid during that year and the 1911 report includes an item of £766 for 'renewals in permanent way'. In his articles in the *Railway Magazine* for 1912 on the railway, 'F.S.W.' indicates that the renewals were still going on at that time. He says '. . . the present rails are 42 lb. to the yard which are however being replaced by 60 lb. rails'. A.R. Bennett in the article quoted above says, '. . . the original rails were only 32 lb. to the yard; later they were replaced by others of 42 lb. to the yard, and the line is now being relaid with 60 lb. rails. . . .' Note that 'now' means 1927, only four years before the closure. It seems also that the original company laid down sleepers which were, says L. Gatt, 'of common fir and not creosoted'. Government laid 12,000 new oak creosoted sleepers.

In the reports, it is difficult sometimes to separate, in financial terms, the laying of new track from the normal work of maintenance, and equally difficult as already pointed out above to decide whether or not there was excessive expenditure on permanent way. What can be said with certainty is that the railway never had a serious accident. Derailments were rare and generally confined to track other than the main line. Many people still alive who were regular passengers have remarked upon the smoothness of travel.

Manning, Wardle 2-6-4T No. 6 poses for the photographer with its heavily laden train at Hamrun *circa* 1910. The engine shed is just visible behind the train. The carbide lamp was a permanent feature. It was never removed to bunker service.

John Alsop Collection

As one would expect, coal was expensive. The bill for 1908 was £1,430, for 1911 £1,200 and for 1931 £1,865. Buhagiar (the Manager from 1897) had viewed with some anxiety this high expenditure on coal and as early as 1903 he reported that,

> . . . the saving on the expenditure for coal during the year by the use of the briquette manufactured at the railway yard is estimated at £308, and it is hoped that a higher sum will be saved next year owing to the new and improved press which has been constructed at the Hamrun Yard for the manufacture of briquette.

In 1911 he says, somewhat plaintively,

> I may add that but for the fact that the price of coal ruled high, the increase in this year's expenditure, as compared with that of 1909-10, would have amounted to only £80, notwithstanding the outlay on the construction of the stations at Attard and Birchircara.

The uniforms issued to the staff followed the conventional and contemporary patterns. There was both summer and winter wear. Photographs taken during the period 1900-1920 show senior uniformed staff as being very smartly turned out, collectors having stiff white winged collars with black tie, and a peaked cap. Buttons were embossed with the Government cypher.

How then did the railway under Government fare financially? In the 1904 report the following figures were quoted:

	1902-3 £.	s.	d.	1903-4 £.	s.	d.
1. Capital expended by Government for the re-equipment of the Railway to date	39,524	2	4	39,690	9	6
2. Gross Revenue	9,020	5	7¾	9,272	13	4
3. Working expenses	6,105	9	4½	6,043	4	0
4. Interest	1,122	3	10	1,128	16	6
5. Renewals	530	16	10¾	1,483	4	1
6. Capital unexpended	1,261	15	6½	617	8	9
7. Number of passengers	924,350			959,130		

It is apparent that at this period Government was prepared to advance capital to the railway in accordance with its policy of keeping the line alive. This was very reasonable because in these two years 1,883,480 passengers were carried, when the total population of the islands was less than 300,000 and the catchment area was 100,000 or 15,000 per mile of line.

The following figures throw further light on to the financial positions:

	1907 s. d.	1908 s. d.	1910 s. d.	1911 s. d.	1930 s. d.	1931 s. d.
Total earnings per train mile	1 11¾	2 0¼	1 7½	1 5¼	1 9¾	1 5¼
Total working expenses per train mile	1 7¾	1 6¾	1 5¾	1 4¾	3 6	3 4¼
	+4¾	+5½	+1¾	+½	−1 8¼	−1 11

Figures for the period of World War I and immediately afterwards are not available, but the general trend can be seen. At least until 1911, on these figures and

An evocative scene as Black, Hawthorn 0-6-0ST No. 4 crosses the road just outside Birkirkara station with a train bound for Museum. In this photograph the locomotive is domeless, but her original spark-arresting chimney has been replaced. This scene is thus probably at the turn of the 20th century.

R. Ellis

Railway staff pose with Beyer, Peacock 2-6-4T No. 7 at Museum station. The Bissel truck can be clearly seen.

MALTA RAILWAY.

Bearer *Rev. Geo: Maria Cachia*
is allowed to travel in third class
carriages at reduced fares by the Railway
between Valletta and *Attard* from
the 1st October 1908, until further orders.

Manager & Engineer.

(See over)

A railway pass for a parish priest   *Colling Turner & Cyril Smith*

Beyer, Peacock 2-6-4T No. 7 waits to leave Notabile station in 1915 with a train for Valletta.
John Alsop Collection

within itself, the undertaking was solvent. As many troop trains were run during the years 1914-18, in addition to normal services, we may assume that solvency continued until trams and buses began, from the end of the war onwards, to undermine the railway. The figures for 1930 and 1931 support these assumptions.

It is illuminating, against these figures to look again at the passengers per year. They remained surprisingly constant at around 900,000 per year showing that the railway maintained a traditional popularity throughout its life, until the catastrophic drop in the last two years or so due to bus competition. Increases in fares seem never to have been considered.

'F.S.W.' in 1912 in the *Railway Magazine* said,

> . . . the company having failed to make the line pay, Government were however quite successful and began to make money in spite of the fact that there was little goods traffic until tramways were introduced into the island.

This was the situation right up to the closing of the line. Government considered, very rightly, that it was a public amenity and were prepared to give financial support if losses were not too great. However, they expected and obtained the utmost initiative and effort from the Manager and his staff in extracting the greatest possible value for money expended.

The full report for the year 1907-8 from Buhagiar gives a detailed insight into the workings of the line, and included the following:

> The increase in the revenue is due partly to heavier traffic to Notabile, and partly to the fact that more special trains were run than in the preceding year.
>
> The amount expended on renewals was £1,814 15s. 2½d. which, compared with the amount expended in 1906-7, shows a decrease of £1,084 15s. 10½d. The expenditure on renewals in 1906-7 was above the average, two engine boilers having been purchased in that year.
>
> No additions to the rolling stock were made during the year, but locomotives Nos. 1, 4, 9 and nine carriages were overhauled and painted.
>
> As in previous years, the work done on the permanent way included the reconstruction of a portion of the line and the laying of new and heavier rails and sleepers; the raising and levelling of the embankments, the construction of retaining walls, the laying of new ballast, and the draining of the line.

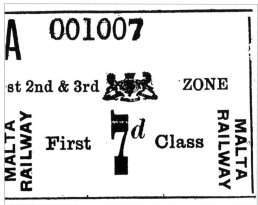

All tickets were produced on thin paper.   *Colling Turner & Cyril Smith*

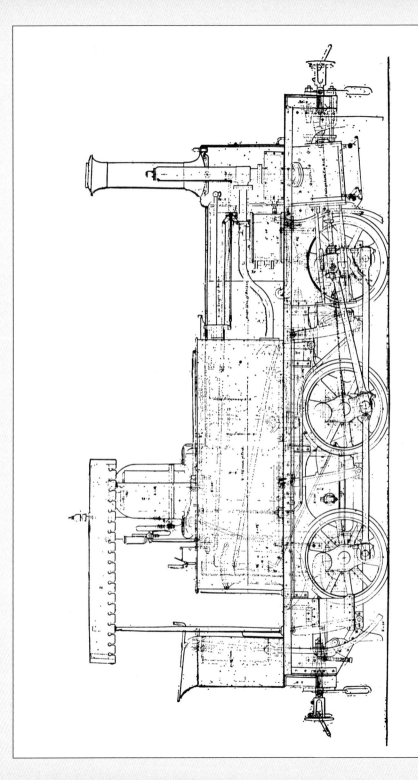

General arrangement drawing of Manning, Wardle 0-6-0T locomotive No. 1.

Chapter Four

The Locomotives and Rolling Stock

The Locomotives

There were 10 locomotives: the railway did not officially classify them. However, there were three classes, and if we call them I, II and III in chronological order, Class I may be subdivided (i) Nos. 1, 2 and 3, and (ii) No. 4: Class II includes Nos. 5 and 6 and Class III 7, 8, 9 and 10. There has always been - and still is - a belief in Malta that the locomotives and rolling stock came second-hand from the Isle of Wight, presumably from the railways on that island. This of course was not so.

The list was as follows:

No.	Type	Maker	Maker's No.	Date Built
1	0-6-0T	Manning, Wardle & Co. Ltd, Leeds	842	1882
2	0-6-0T	Manning, Wardle & Co. Ltd, Leeds	843	1882
3	0-6-0T	Manning, Wardle & Co. Ltd, Leeds	844	1883
4	0-6-0ST	Black, Hawthorn and Co. Ltd, Gateshead	753	1884
5	2-6-2T	Manning, Wardle & Co. Ltd, Leeds	1243	1891
6	2-6-4T	Manning, Wardle & Co. Ltd, Leeds	1261	1892
7	2-6-4T	Beyer, Peacock & Co. Ltd, Manchester	3678	1895
8	2-6-4T	Beyer, Peacock & Co. Ltd, Manchester	3852	1896
9	2-6-4T	Beyer, Peacock & Co. Ltd, Manchester	4163	1899
10	2-6-4T	Beyer, Peacock & Co. Ltd, Manchester	4719	1903

The list presents an interesting cameo of the invention and development in England of the narrow gauge steam locomotive in its critical early decades. In terms of profile alone there is a great difference between No. 1 and No. 10 of the Malta Railway. Both are attractive in their different ways and No. 1 was a splendid little workhorse whereas one or two of the later engines became rather more decorative than enthusiastic.

The builders' names are famous in the locomotive world. The history is a complicated one as there were many mergers over the years with the development of the industry. The emergence in Great Britain of the large standard gauge companies revealed the workings of the economies of scale, so that a company would, say, order 10 locomotives from a private firm and build a further 30 in its own workshops. One sees this tendency in our little Malta Railway, where quite advanced workshops were set up at Hamrun, although they never actually built a locomotive.

An examination of the locomotive building firms in the list reveals well-known and highly respected firms in the industry. They also enjoyed working in the narrow gauge (of which there was more than one definition) not least because the building of railways in many countries embraced the narrow gauge, as it was cheaper to build and run than the standard. The works were located in the North of England and in Scotland.

Works photograph of Manning, Wardle 0-6-0T locomotive No. 1, carrying its Works number, 842, on its plate.

Manning, Wardle 0-6-0T No. 2 in April 1927 with modifications. *A. Pisani*

Neither the Government nor Mr Buhagiar would have dreamt of buying their locomotives from anywhere else than the United Kingdom, in spite of a growing expertise in this field in the continent of Europe. Nos. 1, 2 and 3 were bought by the Government from Manning, Wardle in the 1880s. This firm began life in 1858 in Leeds when it took over the failed but historically important E.B. Wilson. Manning, Wardle was to last until 1927. Apart from the blip in the purchase of No. 4 (to which we later refer) the Malta Railway remained faithful to Manning, Wardle (Nos. 5, 6 and 7) until 1892 when it turned to Beyer, Peacock of Manchester who began business in 1854.

Mr Buhagiar, always dapper in appearance, sporting a boater and a bow-tie, saw to it that his little railway met his own standards of what a military man would call a 'smart turnout'. He watched the developments in locomotive design over the years so that when it became economically possible and desirable to purchase new locomotive stock, he turned to the elegant engines of the late 19th century and as we can see, to those two companies - Manning, Wardle and Beyer, Peacock. It could be argued that 10 locomotives were more than enough for the running of the railway; however the timetable was quite intensive and there were also many special trains, taking citizens to and from the religious festivals in the various villages and small towns. Interwoven into this social fabric was the Malta Railway.

The Malta Railway began the service with Nos. 1, 2 and 3. The company was to buy one more - No. 4 in 1884 - before Government took over. In their first few years of life with the company, the locomotives had a miserable time due to neglect. In consequence they had to undergo considerable repairs and renovation in the Dockyards at the end of the 1880s. Nevertheless, these little machines gave long and excellent service. They were traditional features of the line from the first day almost to the last. They were popular with the drivers because of their terrier-like abilities and the simplicity of their working. There was an excellent all-round view from the cab in each of these engines. The drivers liked to see what was going on around and about, in true Maltese fashion. One driver told us that he would stop his train for a few moments when passing the Mile End sports stadium, '. . . if there was anything exciting happening'. The open canopy roof was fashionable for railways in the sun at this period.

The principal dimensions of Nos. 1-3 were:

Outside cylinders	10½ in. x 18 in.
Wheelbase	9 ft 7 in.
Grate area	4½ sq. ft
Heating surface, firebox	84 sq. ft
tubes	240 sq. ft
Total	324 sq. ft
Tanks	350 galls capacity
Weight, empty	17 tons
full	22 tons

The locomotives were originally fitted with a special feed-water heating arrangement. This system continued in use for some years without any

Black, Hawthorn 0-6-0ST No. 4 in original condition, as a saddle tank with a spark arrestor chimney.

No. 4 in her final form as a side tank. The spark arrestor was removed at the time of her coversion from a saddle tank. This photograph was taken at Hamrun at the auction in 1931 after the railway's closure.   *A. Pisani*

apparent benefit, and was removed when injectors came to be substituted for the original feed-pumps. In 1906 all three engines were fitted with new boilers. These were replicas of the old ones except that the boiler barrels and tubes were made six inches longer, presumably because the Manager considered that experience warranted the additions. The boilers must surely have come from Manning, Wardle although it has not been possible to verify this presumption. This is interesting because by 1906 the railway had bought its tenth and last locomotive and had transferred its custom to other manufacturers. It is of even further interest that the Hamrun shops were already capable, in the early 1900s, of major maintenance and engineering work.

It was not until 1927 that No. 3 became beyond economical repair and began to be used as a reserve of spare parts for the other two. For more than two decades these busy little locomotives were to be seen taking trains of five or six carriages up the 1 in 60 bank out of Valletta as far as Birkirkara and - once a day - four carriages up the 1 in 40 bank to Notabile. Nos. 1, 2 and 3 carried spark arresting baskets during the summer months.

No. 4, as already mentioned, was unique. This locomotive had been ordered by the company, before Government took over. The works photograph appears in the catalogue of Chapman & Furneaux, who were the successors to Black, Hawthorn & Company Ltd. It is not clear why there was a change from Manning, Wardle to Chapman & Furneaux. Obviously there had been a decision that No. 4 should be a more powerful engine than the first three. But she was still 0-6-0 and her type could well have been ordered from Manning Wardle, especially in view of the proved ability of the Manning, Wardles to stand up to hard work - and neglect. But Chapman & Furneaux it was, and it transpired that this was to be the only one from them. One supposes that if No. 4 had proved satisfactory, more of her class would have been ordered. Meantime, Government took over and the new managers had ideas beyond 0-6-0s. The dimensions of No. 4 were as follows:

Cylinders (2)	13 in. x 19 in.
Coupled wheels diameter	3 ft 2 in.
Wheelbase, rigid and total	11 ft 6 in.
Tanks (saddle) capacity	620 gallons
Bunker capacity	38 cu. ft
Total heating surface	498 sq. ft
Grate area	8½ sq. ft
Minimum curve radius	130 ft
Weight, full	23 tons
empty	18 tons, 15 cwt

Loaded hauls exclusive of locomotive at 12/15 mph	
On level	568 tons
Up 1 in 25 gradient	61 tons
Minimum weight of rail per yard	48 lb.
Tractive power	8,872 lb.

As supplied she was equipped, according to her makers, 'with a powerful handbrake', a spark-arresting chimney and feed-water heater. The latter system

General arrangement drawing of Manning, Wardle 2-6-2T locomotive No. 5.

was subsequently removed as in the cases of Nos. 1 to 3. From the beginning of her working life No. 4 was a cause for some concern, and the Manager, Mr L. Gatt, did not conceal his dislike of her. She was not so steady on the rails as the first three. This unsteadiness was ascribed to the saddle-tank which was thought to make her top heavy. She had arrived for duty in 1884 and thus had some six years of company life until the line closed in 1890. When the Hamrun shops were developed and extended by Government, No. 4 was one of the first major locomotive jobs to be tackled. She was converted to side tanks; at the same time her spark-arresting chimney was removed and a smart cylindrical brass-bound one was substituted. A dome was added; also a number plate in the style of the railway, i.e. a brass oval plate with 'No. 4' embossed within, the background painted in red. The maker's name plate, large and oval-shaped, engraved 'Black and Hawthorn Ltd. No. 753. Engineers. Gateshead-on-Tyne', was removed from the front side-panels of the cab (because these panels disappeared when the side tanks were installed) and put on to the rear panels. When finally in 1907 she was re-boilered her appearance had changed tremendously from that at her debut. One cannot help feeling that poor No. 4 was the guinea pig in the early days when everyone was wanting to try out his skill as a locomotive engineer.

Apparently she never really 'steadied up'. Nevertheless she was a well-liked little engine, over whom a lot of trouble was taken and she settled down to a lengthy working life (although she was out of service for most of 1919 with a cracked cylinder) as the general purposes engine of the line with the reputation of a tireless worker.

For the next two engines, Nos. 5 and 6, Government turned to Manning, Wardle, the firm that had supplied the first three to the Malta Railway Company Ltd. The designs and specifications for 5 and 6 were supplied by the Crown Agents for the Colonies and represented a considerable development in power from the little 0-6-0s. It is interesting too to note the position taken up by the Crown Agents as liaison officers for the pooling and spreading of ideas in, and experience of, locomotive design in the Colonies.

No. 5 as supplied was a 2-6-2 side tank whose leading dimensions were as follows:

Cylinders (2)	15 in. x 20 in.
Leading bogie wheels diameter	2 ft 2 in.
Coupled wheels diameter	3 ft 3 in.
Trailing radial axle wheels diameter	2 ft 9 in.
Total wheelbase	21 ft 6 in. (of which 8 ft 6 in. were rigid)
Heating surface	754 sq. ft (71 sq. ft in firebox)
Tank capacity	1,000 gallons
Grate area	10 sq. ft
Weight in working order	39 tons

That the Manager was aiming at a considerable increase in power when compared with the first four locomotives is shown by the cylinder and heating surface dimensions. She arrived in Malta early in 1892 and on being set to work it was found that she was causing considerable damage to the permanent way.

These two images show the contrast between the Manning, Wardle 2-6-2T No. 5 (Works No. 1243) built in 1891, and No. 6 (Works No. 1261) the 2-6-4T from the following year from the same maker.

Further, according to one writer, she was also unsatisfactory because her wheelbase was too rigid; this is an interesting criticism in view of the dimensions quoted above. Mr Stellin mentions that the heavy coal consumption of No. 5 (and No. 6) was in his view another important factor in their relegation to semi-retirement. He says, 'they were heavy duty locomotives and were used only for emergency purposes, i.e. when other engines were on repair'.

It seems to have been decided that there was too much weight on the trailing axle and that this was the cause of her breaking up the track. A four-wheeled trailing bogie was ordered from Manning, Wardle (1900 in their books, but possibly actually ordered earlier) and instructions given that No. 6 was to be a 2-6-4T. The new bogie for No. 5 was fitted at the Hamrun shops after the frame had been lengthened at the bunker end at the shop. All this increased the total wheelbase to 25 ft 9 in. and the working weight to 41 tons, as well as increasing the water capacity.

There are differing reports about the date of arrival of No. 6; it was most probably 1892. Her dimensions were essentially the same as the rebuilt No. 5, the main difference being that the tank capacity was reduced to 1,025 gallons because an inspection aperture was made. The general arrangement drawings for No. 6 show two heights of chimney and two positions for the dome. Both Nos. 5 and 6 had rectangular ports. Both locomotives carried large headlamps placed in front of the funnel. They were acetylene lamps and the carbide used was known to the Maltese drivers as 'grey coal'. The lamps remained permanently in front. When the engines were travelling bunker first, an ordinary oil lamp was positioned at the top centre of the rear bunker panel.

It is probable that the reason for the unsuccessful working of Nos. 5 and 6 was simply the bad luck of their being just that little bit too heavy for the permanent way at the time when they were put on it. The permanent way was constantly being strengthened and the rails made heavier and heavier per foot length. The later successful locomotives were all slightly heavier than Nos. 5 and 6, yet these later engines did not damage the track. Later on in the lives of Nos. 5 and 6, therefore, they should not in theory have done any damage to the track and should have begun successful running, but once they went into semi-retirement they remained in that state. The high quality and general all-round usefulness of the earlier engines served to accentuate the disappointment felt about Nos. 5 and 6. These had long periods of complete idleness but were always kept in first-class condition. It is difficult to resist the conclusion that they were used for technical school work rather than railway, because they were very good engines and could surely have been used with safety on the later tracks.

They were 'on shed' for stray photographers over the years and they are pictured in most of the articles on the railway that were published during its lifetime. A postcard (copies of which can still be had in Mdina and elsewhere) shows either 5 or 6 in Museum station in about 1912. Mr Buhagiar is standing on the platform together with a group of soldiers of the 2nd Scottish Rifles and railway workers. No. 6 was withdrawn from regular working in 1914 and No. 5 in 1920, but for both engines there had been several considerable gaps in their regular duties.

It was the view of Mr A.R. Bennett, writing in *The Locomotive* in 1927, that the trouble with Nos. 5 and 6 was '. . . that the advanced position of the leading axle

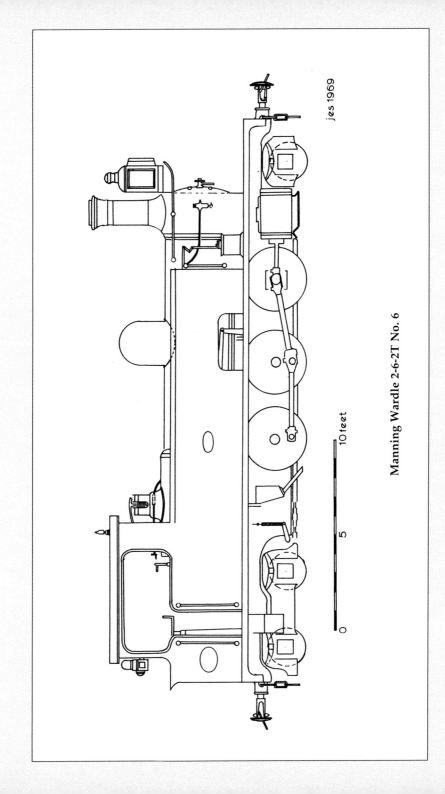

Manning Wardle 2-6-2T No. 6

jœs 1969

10 feet

5

0

and the extension forward of the big water tank throws an excessive weight on the coupled wheels'. There was quality and efficiency in these two engines in spite of the view which seems to have been taken of them. There are apparently no records of either having actually failed on duty. They had graceful lines, showing the style that marked British narrow-gauge design at this time and which in the case of the Malta Railway was to be seen also in the last four locomotives ordered from Beyer, Peacock.

Mr Stellin says of these last four that 'they were very beautiful in appearance'; something that he has remembered for nearly 40 years. It will be appreciated that the railway had had to rely upon Nos. 1-4 for some three years longer than had been expected. Mr Buhagiar - and the Crown Agents for the Colonies - were obviously now convinced that 2-6-4 tanks with a smaller rigid wheelbase than Nos. 5 and 6 were what was required.

Beyer, Peacock delivered No. 7 in 1895 to the order of the Crown Agents. The firm had much experience in this design and No. 7 was a replica (less cow-catcher and steam-sanding apparatus) of an engine they had supplied in 1893 to the Minas and Rio Railway.

The principal dimensions were:

Cylinders		14¼ in. x 20 in.
Leading and trailing bogie wheels diameter		2 ft 0⅛ in.
Coupled wheels diameter		3 ft 3⅜ in.
Total wheelbase		23 ft 2 in.
Rigid wheelbase		7 ft 6 in.
Boiler barrel		9 ft 1 in. length
Tubes		160 ft, 1⅞ in.
Grate area		12 sq. ft
Heating surface firebox		65.4 sq. ft
tubes		635.3 sq. ft
	Total	700.7 sq. ft
Working pressure		160 lb. psi
Weight in working order		
Front bogie		4 tons 1 cwt
Coupled wheels		19 tons 16 cwt
Rear bogie		11 tons 14 cwt
	Total	35 tons 11 cwt
Tank capacity		
Side tanks		600 gallons
Bunker tank		400 gallons
	Total	1,000 gallons
Fuel capacity		32 cwt level
		40 cwt piled up

The cylinders were placed over the wheels of a Bissel truck at an inclination of 1 in 8½, a feature well-known through the same company's engines for the Isle of Man Railway.

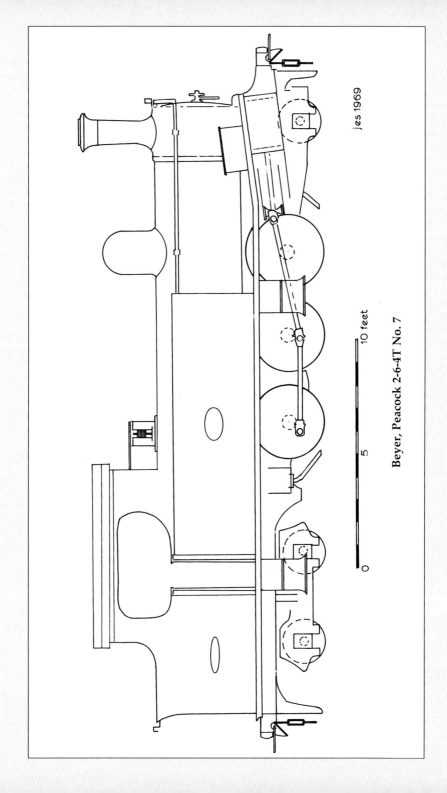

Beyer, Peacock 2-6-4T No. 7

10 feet

5

0

jes 1969

No. 7 outside Hamrun shed, shortly after delivery in 1895.

A. Pisani

Beyer, Peacock 2-6-4T No. 9 was delivered to the railway in 1899.

No. 10 outside Hamrun shed in the 1920s. *A. Pisani*

It will be seen that the general plan for the remaining locomotives was not dissimilar to that for Nos. 5 and 6, and in spite of the disappointments experienced with these two engines it was felt that they had set the pattern for the future of the line. Of course, there were differences. To begin with, the load distribution of No. 7 was different from 5 and 6. The weight of the cylinders and the front part of the engine was now carried by the Bissel truck and by transferring 400 gallons of water to a bunker tank a considerable load was thus removed from the side tanks and the coupled wheels. In fact these latter locomotives were carrying less on their coupled wheels than Nos. 1-4 had done. No. 7 rode easily and smoothly and from the beginning was accepted as satisfactory. Three more engines of the same design were subsequently delivered and the total stud of 10 served the line until its closure in 1931. Nos. 7, 8, 9 and 10 carried out most of the work in the last decade and all four were re-boilered at Hamrun at different times. No. 9 was often to be seen in summer carrying water-tanks on wagons to the villages.

Some doubts were later expressed as to whether the reduction on the coupled wheels had not been carried too far. Traffic on festival days and holidays tended to be so heavy and concentrated as sometimes to require more than the 12 coaches per train, which was the most they could handle on the long climb from Attard onwards to the terminus. In making this point A.R. Bennett says, 'an additional 2 or 3 tons of adhesion would be acceptable'. But D. Stellin says simply that 'they performed wonderfully well'. During World War I troop trains of more than 12 coaches per train were common. They ran non-stop from Valletta to Museum and vice versa, usually hauled by one of the Beyer, Peacocks and with a banker. No. 4, the sturdy maid of all work, was familiar in the supporting role.

The locomotive livery was a dark olive green with black smokebox and vermilion buffer beams. The domes were brass and chimneys had copper bands at the tops. Wheels and frames were black. Each engine carried a brass oval number plate located in the centre of the side tank. The plate had a red painted background and the number was raised in brass thus: 'No. 6'. On some of the engines there was also a maker's name plate in the centre of the bunker panel. The original Malta Railway Company Limited had a seal, which consisted of the Maltese Cross with a circular surrounding strap garter containing the words 'Malta Railway Company Ltd.' This was never adapted into a crest and the later Malta Railway did not have a crest. When the locomotives were delivered they were lined out on tank-sides, cab-panels and boiler strappings. It is not possible now to say what these linings were and photographs show that they were not uniform in design. But it appears that as they came into shops for repainting, the linings were not repeated, whether for reasons of economy or indifference is not known.

All locomotives were kept in smart and tidy trim until the last few years, when standards deteriorated. Nos. 1, 2, 3 and 4 cost rather more than £1,000 each, and Nos. 5 and 6 just over £2,000 each. It has not been possible to trace the costs of 7, 8, 9 and 10, but in all probability they would have cost about between £2,500 and £3,000 each.

Third class carriage

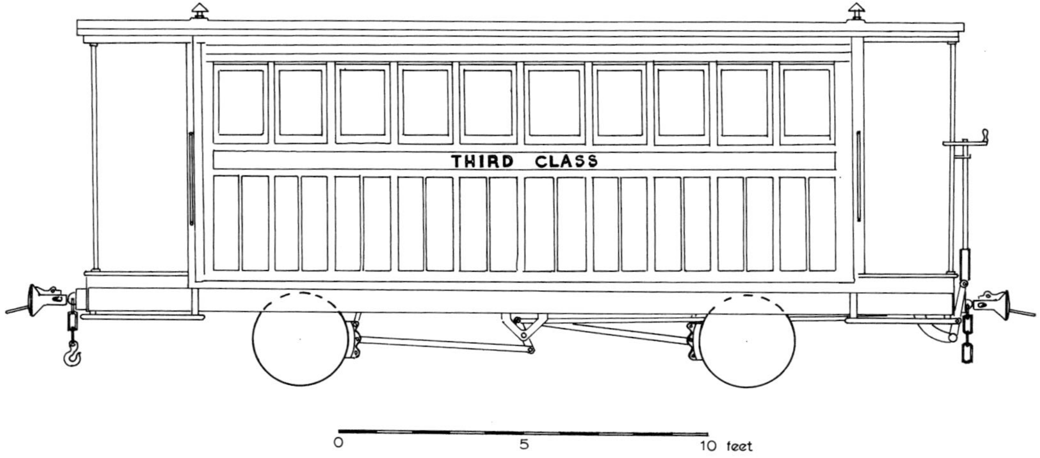

Workmen's carriage

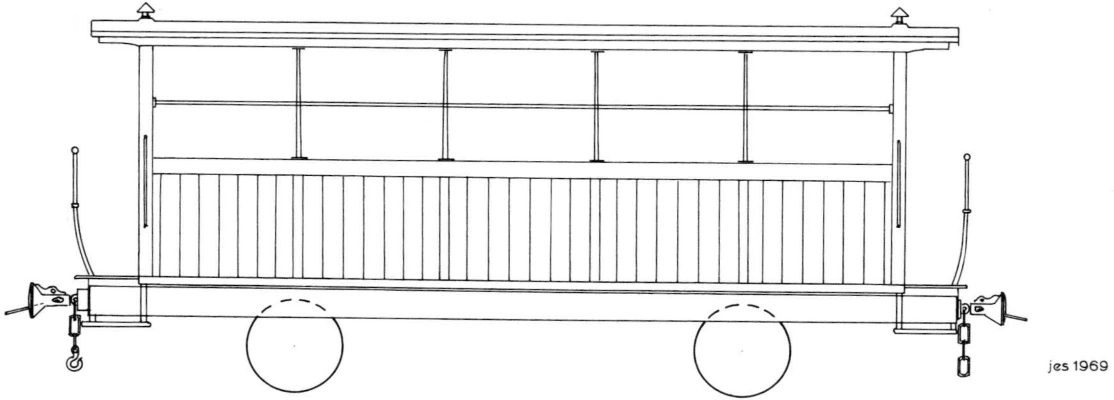

10 feet

5

0

jes 1969

The Rolling Stock

There were, at maximum, 33 passenger coaches, a lesser number of workmen's carriages, and a very small number, probably less than 12, ballast wagons and platelayers' trolleys. The company kept their coaches in the open, but under Government sheds were provided at Hamrun.

The writer describing the opening ceremony mentions seven carriages. From this beginning of seven in 1883 to 33 in 1931 the passenger coaches and workmen's carriages remained essentially unchanged in design, that is four-wheeled wooden vehicles with steel chassis and fixtures. Even when the line was transporting hundreds of thousands of passengers every year these simple vehicles were able to handle the traffic. Some obvious advantages spring immediately to mind. They were easily capable of negotiating the many bends (maximum curve 10 chains radius), could be wholly maintained in the Hamrun shops and were inexpensive in upkeep. Their short individual lengths enabled them to be made up into malleable rakes, they were easy to store and adaptable to local movement for 'making-up'. A driver with many years' experience of the line has said that the rule of thumb amongst drivers was that Nos. 1, 2 and 3 took four to five coaches, No. 4, five to six coaches and the remainder up to 10. Some writers, however, have said that Nos. 7, 8, 9 and 10 could each manage 12. At any rate let us say that there was a maximum of coaches, most probably 10, above which it was normal to give Nos. 7, 8, 9 and 10 the help of a second locomotive in the rear. It should of course be appreciated that the assistance of an engine in the rear for a 10-plus train going up to Valletta (i.e. downhill) was just as important from the control point of view as for a train going down to Museum (i.e. uphill). There were no continuous brakes.

When coaches were made up into a train, connecting planks, slotted into free-running channels, enabled ticket sellers and inspectors to get from one coach to the next and so conduct their business. Coaches, like locomotives, had one central spring buffer to each end beam. At the beginning there were first, second and third classes (some coaches were composite), in addition to 'workmen's'. After a short time, probably from the take-over by Government, the system became first, third and workmen's. Until 1900 all passenger coaches were lit by candle. There was a carefully regulated system by which officials up and down the line were charged with the duties of lighting or snuffing candles depending upon the time of day and the proximity of tunnel. Most probably the man on duty, in earlier days at least, did this by means of lighted taper and snuffer. Later on it was a matter of a box of matches and a puff!

The picture thus conjured up is both intriguing and incongruous. The 1880s and 1890s were, after all, years in which such an arrangement might well have been thought outdated. But to the Maltese passengers, of course, the railway was both new and astonishing; and they were quite used to seeing, almost every day, candles being lighted and snuffed in their churches.

One finds the social structure of the line contained an interesting combination of traditional British railway practice and local adaptation and custom. The scrapping of second class, indeed the concept of class division by coaches; the idea of special workmen's trains; vermilion buffer beams; all these are examples of similarities and differences. Some coaches, if not all, had nicknames; one was called 'Iz-Zugraga' - 'The Top'.

Workmen's carriage of the type designed by Metropolitan Carriage & Wagon Co.   *A. Pisani*

Workmen's carriage of the type designed by Swansea Wagon Co. These photographs were taken at the time of the auction in 1931 at Hamrun.   *A. Pisani*

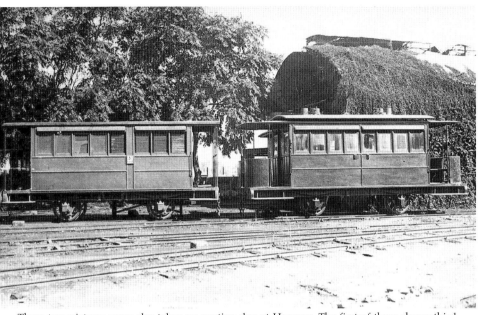

These two pictures were also taken on auction day at Hamrun. The first of these shows third class (*left*) and first class (*right*) carriages of Swansea Wagon Co. origin.   *A. Pisani*

This view shows a third class Metropolitan Carriage & Wagon Co.-built vehicle. To the left is a ballast wagon.   *A. Pisani*

Another view from the auction day at Hamrun in 1931 shows, *left*, Lot 3 Schedule B first class carriage and, *right*, Lot 7 Schedule B third class carriage. Both vehicles are of Swansea Wagon Company origin.

A. Pisani

The third class coaches weighed 6 tons each. They were 23 ft long over the headstocks, 15 ft wide and 10 ft high. Accommodation has been variously quoted as between 24 and 28 persons; the plans say 26. However, according to a contemporary writer 'as passengers are allowed to stand on the platforms and also strap hang in the carriages, the carrying capacity is often demonstrably greatly in excess of the seating'.

From the end verandahs, entrance to the saloon was gained through doors with glass top-frames. There was a circular 'spy glass' window in the top of the wall on either side of the door and 10 windows lengthwise on either side of the coach. Photographs show, however, that this was not invariable, some coaches having eight windows lengthwise on either side. There were ventilating louvres above the windows and also 'let-down' louvres for the windows themselves, the 'let-downs' in practice being little used. In hot weather the passengers preferred letting the glass windows down into their panel slots, in order to admit as much air as possible into the coaches. Within the saloon the seats ran lengthwise on either side, as in the English tramcar of the period. They were indeed carried out in the 'tramcar' style, that is light yellow wooden sprung-panels with polka-dot patterns incised upon them and with mahogany finished frameworks. The very wide central passage gave room for many standing passengers. The end verandahs also invariably had their quotas of standing passengers during rush hours. There were luggage racks above the seats and four ventilators in the roof.

At one end of the coach, running up beside and secured to the verandah strapping, was the handbrake gear. This, topped by the usual horizontally placed wheel with handle fixed to the circumference, applied shoe brakes to all four wheels. The officials travelling in the train, and the drivers, had over the years worked out a close co-ordination of brake applications for the control of their trains. For example a driver gave three short whistles if he wished the conductor to apply the brakes. Although the gradient profile gave the impression that there were some apparently formidable problems of braking, it should be remembered that the main line was only about seven miles long and it would, therefore, be possible for officials to memorise stretches of it in great detail. Nevertheless, it is remarkable that no runaway was ever recorded in the history of the railway. The coach bearing-springs were 8-plated 3 in. x ½ in.

During the 'candle' period, third class coaches had only two candles, one in each opposite diagonal corner, contained in a framed recess 10 in. x 1 ft 4 in. and labelled on the original plans, somewhat optimistically, 'lamp'.* When electricity was introduced in 1900, 8-cell storage batteries were placed two under each seat within the saloon and bulbs were placed at intervals along the length of the saloon ceiling. The livery was dark olive green, with the words 'Third Class' in white lettering on the panels immediately beneath the windows and arranged in balanced form on either side of the vertical centre line of the coach. In all cases undercarriages were black.

The first class coaches were similar in design to the third class. The verandahs were, however, nearly twice as deep and had a closed-in surround (rather like a tramcar) that reached round to each step-entrance. There were four outside seats of varnished teak on each verandah, one in each corner. The first class saloon thus seated 18 instead of 26 passengers as in the third class, and there

* Mr Lawrence, in the caption to his photograph on page 95 says that there was an interim period during which oil lamps were use.

An end view of the Governor's saloon in Hamrun sidings.   *A. Pisani*

were eight windows on each side as against the normal 10. The two length-wise seats in the saloon had the additional luxury of being cushion-covered. First class passengers considered themselves greatly privileged in having the eight outside seats. It was here where nannies could be found with their charges and senior government officials sat with businessmen from Valletta enjoying the coolness of the breeze as the train moved out from the city to the suburbs. The coach livery for first class was varnished teak with the words 'First Class' in gold lettering on the panels immediately beneath the windows and arranged in balanced form on either side of the vertical centre line of the coach.

H.E. The Governor's coach was similar in general design to the first class coaches. With its cushions and plush-lined seats and brocade curtains, it was a period piece that survived into the 1930s and it is sad to think it has not been preserved.

The lighting of H.E.'s coach was by storage batteries as in the first class coaches but there was in addition an axle-mounted generator. The batteries took over when the generator cut off.

This vehicle was an integral part of the railway scene as it made its important progress to St Anton from Valletta behind a trim little green 0-6-0 with copper-bound funnel, polished brass dome and vermilion buffer beams. Sometimes the journey would be to Notabile or Museum, there to call upon distinguished citizens in Mdina or military friends a little further afield.

As a contrast to all this, the workmen's carriages, 20 ft 5 in. long, were austere affairs. This class of vehicle was a feature from the opening of the line and obviously the private company used it at Government request. There were several variations of the general pattern, between Geneste's original and the Hamrun final. The intermediates were built by Oldbury & Co. and Swansea Wagon. The original drawings, signed by F.A.B. Geneste in July 1883, show a four-wheeled vehicle with four compartments containing wooden seats arranged as in an English compartment. Doors and side panels, all in teak, were 3 ft high and the remainder to the roof was open to the elements. Calico curtains were, however, provided, working on rings and rods. For the Maltese climate this was an eminently sensible arrangement.

The workmen's carriage later provided by Government was supposed to be an improvement on that previously provided by the company. There were very narrow end verandahs with no protective surrounds other than a framework of metal tubing. The saloon with central doorways at each end was designed to seat 40 passengers on wooden slatted seats placed cross-wise and back to back in nests of eight with pairs at each end and on either side. There were no windows. The carriage was indeed open to the elements on either side. There were, however, rain curtains which unfurled downwards when required. There was much less space for standing than in the other classes but this did not of course prevent the passengers from 'packing in' when the occasions so warranted.

These vehicles did not possess brakes and it was, therefore, necessary always to include a third class coach in a rake of workmen's carriages so that the regulations for the control of a train in motion could be observed. The livery of the workmen's carriages was an unrelieved battleship grey.

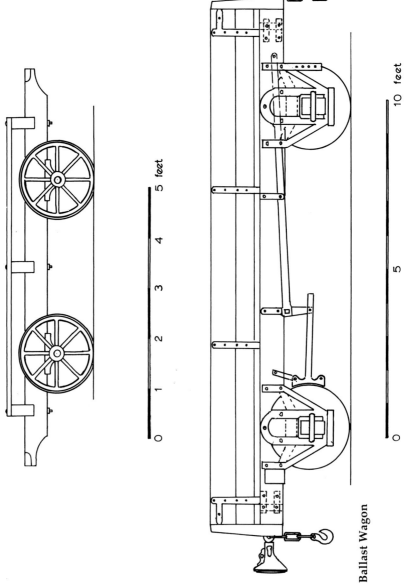

Platelayers' Trolley

Ballast Wagon

jes 1969

5 feet

0 1 2 3 4 5

0 5 10 feet

The interior of a Malta Railway 4-wheel carriage body preserved at Birkirkara station in 1998. Lighting was originally by candle, and later paraffin lamps. The electric light fitting is a recent acquisition.   *A.M. Lawrence*

Trains to Valletta carried a steel box in the charge of the travelling inspector. The public could post letters into this box. It was not necessary to be a passenger on the train before posting. Lengths of chain were suspended from the buffer beams of all coaches, one length immediately on either side of the central buffer. These were coupling links and Dr Graham has vivid recollections from his boyhood of seeing the coupling men carrying out their duties by nipping smartly - and dangerously - in between coaches and out again as they were brought together for service. The ballast wagons were sturdy vehicles built to the traditional pattern. The container was 15 ft 6 in. x 7 ft x 1 ft 6 in., the floor being lined with iron tonguing. A manually operated brake-gear applied a shoe brake to one set of wheels. There was good springing of seven 3 in. x ½ in. plates.

The platelayers' trolleys were very simple vehicles. There were no brakes, axle boxes, buffers or coupling devices. The overall length was 8 ft and width 4 ft 6 in. A platform 6 ft in length and 4 ft 6 in. wide was placed just above the chassis frame and there was a 3 ft 6 in. wheelbase. The trolleys were only 1 ft 9½ in. high. Mr Farrugia remembers 'ballast trolleys' as he called them that could easily be derailed upon the approach of a train and were manhandled along the track, a board being used as a brake! There was always plenty of permanent way work on hand because the standard of track maintenance was high and because sun, wind and rain in Malta are all severe in their effects upon the land. In 1908 there was one foreman platelayer, one assistant and 14 others who were called 'Pointsmen and Labourers'. After the earlier experiences no real trouble ever occurred because of imperfect permanent way. Mr Farrugia recalls only one incident, during his time, of derailment due to faulty track. The earlier coaches were produced at the Saltley, Birmingham premises of the Metropolitan Carriage & Wagon Works, now part of the Metropolitan Cammell Company Limited. In the later life of the railway, vehicles were built at the Hamrun workshops.

A preserved Malta Railway 4-wheel carriage body at Birkirkara station in 1998 in what is now a public garden.   *A.M. Lawrence*

Chapter Five

The Workshops

Although the Kingsgate offices housed the Manager and his assistants, and reports, accounts, timetables and the like were prepared there, the working headquarters of the railway was at Hamrun where the shops and sheds were located.

In the early 1900s, when Nicholas Buhagiar had taken over the management of the line, considerable development took place at Hamrun and Buhagiar reported to Government in 1904 that,

> . . . the enlargement of the workshop at Hamrun has now been completed and the improvements in the buildings and the new appliances added have proved of great advantage both from an economical and an engineering point of view; all works in connection with the repairs of locomotives and carriages being now carried out in a more satisfactory manner and at a cheaper cost than before.

It even became possible to build rolling stock.

The workshops were the birthplace of a most important development not directly connected with the running of the railway. This was the setting up of a Technical School. Just exactly how it all began is uncertain; obviously when Government took over some enterprising person realised that the railway workshops, unique in the island, could be used for the training of apprentices in general engineering. This person was most probably the first Manager, Mr L. Gatt, who says in his first report in 1893 when speaking of the building of a Technical School that,

> . . . the object of this school in connection with the railway, is to lay the foundation of a practical system of technical instruction in a manner which will turn the railway workshop to the best and most economical advantage.

To quote again from the 1904 report,

> . . . the Technical School attached to this Department is still being conducted with advantage to Government and to the community. The average number of apprentices trained at the workshop during the year was 20. Seven of them obtained employment at HM Dockyard and three others with private firms.

In 1908 he reported on 17 apprentices, in 1911 23 and in the final year 1931, 30 were reported upon. The expenditure on the Railway Technical School for 1931 was £445.

In the 20th century, therefore, the Railway Department trained some hundreds of apprentices and Hamrun workshops made an important contribution to the development of technical and technological education in Malta. When the railway closed down in 1931 the Director of Education took over the Central Railway Station (as Hamrun station was rather grandly called) and the workshops. The shops and laid-up stock, including the odd abandoned

95

tramcar, continued to be used for technical instruction by the late Professor F. Nixon until the Technical School was closed down, upon the building of the technical institute and school at Paolo.

The average number of employees at any one time throughout the life of the railway department seems to have been about 70. In 1907-8 for example, the staff included a manager, two clerks, 10 ticket clerks, a storekeeper, six drivers, five 'stokers', a fitter, a foreman platelayer and his assistant, 21 gatekeepers, 14 pointsmen/labourers, a carpenter, a boiler-maker and two porters. The accounts for 1907-8 contain an item of £3 as 'risk money allowance to two clerks'. What were these risks? Perhaps it was because they were involved in jumping on and off trains in motion or passing from one coach to another on a moving train. Note the name 'stokers' not 'firemen'; this may have been because of the strong naval tradition in Malta. There were more gatekeepers than any other form of employee; also the poorest paid, but an attractive job in many ways. As one would expect, there were 'characters' amongst the gatekeepers. As time went on the railway acquired a greater number and variety of skilled tradesmen. A foreman of foundry and a blacksmith, for example, were added. Casual extra labour was employed during very busy periods. Obviously too a considerable amount of day-to-day maintenance was carried out by the apprentices as part of their training.

There is at present a school embracing part of the site (and indeed part of the actual buildings) of two sections of the shops, known as the old foundry and the storage shop. The two sections, adjacent to one another, ran along School Street behind St Paul's Square. The storage shop was used for the raking and cleaning of carriages and for re-charging batteries. The electricity department was next to the storage shop; two connecting leads ran from a switchboard in this department along the length of the storage shop, enabling the daily re-charging of batteries.

The foundry although not large was well equipped and enjoyed the services of expert craftsmen. Typical of these was Joseph Cachia, boilermaker, who for a salary of £65 per year undertook work of a difficult and complicated nature with complete success for many years. There was also a foundry foreman who had under him an assistant apprentice and a blacksmith. In its lifetime the foundry turned out a variety of articles, ranging from brake blocks to lamp-posts.

In the fitters' shop behind the foundry there was a steam engine and a gas engine, the former supplying power for the electricity supply. The gas engine was used only when there were major repairs to be done as the result of possibly an accident. But accidents were very rare indeed on the Malta Railway and mechanical breakdowns of a major character were certainly uncommon. However by 1927, says Mr A.R. Bennett, '. . . all tools are now electrically driven, the original gas engine having been superseded by the engineer's latest hand-maiden. Current is supplied from the Government electricity works'.

Standing beside the gas engine were two generators and a switchboard and in an adjoining room were the fitters' benches. The equipment here included a small lathe, a heavy lathe capable of cylinder boring, wheel-turning and the like and a heavy duty drill press which was also used as a boring mill. Additional installations included another press, a lay-out table, a planing table, a shear and a small lathe. Next in succession in the direction of the station platform were the carpenters' shop and a shop containing a power hammer, forges, vices and a lay-out table. At right angles to School Street runs Railway Avenue and all the shops so far described were contained within the area bounded by these angle lines.

On the other side of the station, behind the up platform, was a building with dining room, washroom, apprentices' locker room and overnight sleeping accommodation for drivers. At the Valletta end of the station a tree-lined area contained the locomotive shed and coal yard.

The shed was a substantial building which probably did not perform quite the functions traditional to those of an English railway, although built with that end in view. It seems at least to have been something of a show piece. When railway photography enthusiasts - a much older race than is generally supposed - visited the line, there was always the picture 'on shed' and in later years Nos. 5 or 6 were invariably featured, seeming to have little to do other than to pose for their portraits. In 48 years of active life and on the evidence of this technical education project alone, the railway can be considered to have played an important part in the industrial and commercial development of Malta in the late 19th and early 20th centuries.

Manning, Wardle 2-6-4T No. 6 with the Manning, Wardle 0-6-0T No. 1 on auction day at Hamrun in 1931. One of the Metropolitan Carriage & Wagon Co. workmen's carriages can just be seen beyond the locomotives. *A. Pisani*

The competition, the tramway opened in 1905. Here we see an electric tramcar *en route* between Valletta and Floriana.   *R. Ellis*

No.1 as scrap at Hamrun in 1943, ironically with a tramcar for company.   *Cyril Smith*

Chapter Six

Competition and Closure

By 1904 the railway had built up its number of passengers per year from 630,000 in 1893 to 960,000. It never again reached this latter figure. The electric tramway was introduced in 1905 and by 1910 the railway figure was down to 750,000.

Three tram routes were established from Valletta to Zebbug, Cospicua and Birkirkara. This new means of transport, it was said at the time, was to run between Valletta, the Three Cities and Zebbug and other parts of the island which were not reached by the railway. The latter part of the statement illustrates not only the fact that the railway was now to miss out on its failure to expand but also that Government did not seem to appreciate that the tramway from Valletta to Birkirkara was in direct competition with the railway. Perhaps of course everyone concerned thought there was sufficient - and diverse - passenger traffic to accommodate both undertakings on the dual route.

On the other hand it has been said that the introduction of the tramway did not of itself cause the death of the railway and that although there was route-duplication in the suburban Floriana-Birkirkara complex this did not cause serious financial hardship to the railway. One source says,

> The failure (of the railway) was due partly to the fact that the system had not been designed on commercial lines, partly because the total demand for transport was still relatively small in the areas served, but mainly because a railway service could not be flexible enough to meet the particular demand that did exist. In 1905 a tramway system, less open to objection on all these grounds, was opened. First the area between Valletta, Msida and Hamrun was served, and later lines were built to Zebbug. Designed for passenger rather than freight carrying, the tramways assisted in the extension of urban influence into the country.

But the railway too was designed for passenger carrying rather than freight, and functioned in many ways as a tramway rather than a railway. There was very little distance between stations and trains could be called down at halts. In general the stations were conveniently situated and as to number of passengers carried, in 1907 there were over 300,000 workmen's tickets alone in spite of the trams. However, the argument that the line 'had not been designed on commercial lines' is true to the extent that Government looked upon it as a social amenity. The Managers, though, always tried to run it on commercial lines. Nevertheless, in 1911 Government held a special inquiry into the losses incurred by the railway.

The tramways undertaking was carried on under a Government concession due to expire in 2002. As with the railway there was an option to purchase, the terms in this case after 30 years from the opening of the system being on a basis of 17 times the average net receipts for the preceding three years, plus 20 per cent for compulsory acquisition. However, unlike the railway, the tramway remained a private company until its cessation in 1929.

Certainly the trams took customers away from the railway. They had even more stops than the railway and indeed were quite prepared to stop anywhere. The trams therefore presented the railway with the idea that they could be faced with opponents in the field of transport. Such an idea was quite a novel one. Hitherto their difficulties had been largely those endemic to any little line, namely professional and administrative problems.

Neither the railway nor the tramway company, the one Government owned and the other privately, realised that the arrival of a four-cylinder 20 hp 17-seater omnibus in the island in 1904 meant the beginning of the end for both companies. This vehicle was built by John I. Thornycroft and Co. Ltd and led to the establishment of the Malta Motor Bus Company. The bus company was immediately poised to achieve what neither the railway company nor the tramway company had managed to do, which was to expand routes quickly over Malta. In 1905 Thornycroft received an order for a 16-seat single-decker, a 36-seat double-decker and a 5 ton lorry. In the years up until World War I all three concerns settled down to competition with one another. The war probably did more harm to the, by now growing number of, small proprietors of motor vehicles than to the tram and railway companies. These two latter both had their rolling stock, well tried and *in situ*. The motor owners were not so favourably placed. The railway prospered during the war years even running a number of troop trains to and from Valletta and Museum, the latter station serving Imtarfa military barracks.

After the war, the development of light and cheap chassis for the internal combustion engine, especially in America, meant that vehicles were imported into the island in a steady stream. The numbers of small owners proliferated, the majority owning one vehicle only and abiding by individual rules of operation and maintenance. This phase in the development of public transport was peculiarly attractive to the Maltese with their flair for individuality and mercantile enterprise. The decorative traditional liveries of boat and cart were perpetuated in the motor bus. Each bus carried - and still does, even if in plastic - its religious picture, miniature electric votive lamp, Sacred Heart, Madonna, or St Christopher. No such decoration, so dear to the Maltese heart, adorned the walls of the staid four-wheeled railway coaches or was to be found above 'the glass' in the engine cabs. Some coaches carried a crisp little notice warning passengers against card sharpers, but any such hopefuls must surely have been experts indeed. One could hardly have got much further than inquiring if a quick hand would be in order before Museum station loomed up through the tunnel.

As the buses poured into Malta the railway continued with the now well tried programme of some 14 full-route up and down trains per day with a handful of partial route trains interposed - quite a concentrated programme of work.

Its utter dependence upon passengers meant that it was very vulnerable to the sort of attack now being mounted by the legion of bus proprietors. To a lesser degree at first, but with much acceleration later, the tramways too began to suffer, after having themselves originally taken some traffic from the railway. Nicholas Buhagiar was well aware of the extreme danger to the continued existence of his railway. There had been talk of electrification of the line at least as early as 1912 and presumably what was in mind was an amalgamation of railway and tramways, and the extension of the joint services on the lines planned way back in the 1880s. But nothing came of all this.

People used the railway for the obvious reasons, getting to and from work, attending the various festivals and holiday occasions and visiting relatives. The regularity of the Maltese calendar induced the regularity of the train timetable. But still the buses advanced. Early in 1929 the Overseas Motor Transport Co. Ltd came along in an endeavour to create order out of the chaos of owners of small numbers of vehicles. Like the Malta Railway Companies of the 1880s, this company had English connections - in this case formed by Commander F.T. Hare who had interests in motor transport in Devon, Cornwall and Jersey. Their first step was to buy up the largest of the small operators, the British Motor Co. Ltd, of Malta, which had a small and very mixed fleet. These were replaced by 30 Thornycroft vehicles fitted with Hall-Lewis bodies, a considerable advance upon anything previously used in the island. The first service introduced was from Floriana to Sliema, thus also providing the first rival to the ferry service across the harbour. This too was a pointed challenge to the railway which, although progressing for its first few miles through a dense conurbation, had never embraced Sliema, the fastest growing of all residential areas in Malta, within its control even although the original plans of the private railway company had had this in mind.

This first bus service was followed by the establishment of routes from Floriana to Kalafrana via Birzebbuga and from Floriana to Cospicua. Thus there was now direct competition with the tramways and furthermore all routes still had various rival buses running on them. The situation again brought up discussions between railway and tramways about amalgamation and the electrification of the railway. Again there was nothing beyond discussion.

The tramways closed down in 1929 and the railway in 1931. The bus services now cover Malta, the 15 or so different route liveries having already become an integral part of the colours of the island. The ubiquitous motor bus is hastening the progress - begun in a small way by the railway and the trams - of breaking down the historical antagonisms between the 20th century Valletta conurbation and the earlier agricultural settlements of which Mdina is the titular head.

273664
MALTA RAILWAY
VALLETTA-MUSEUM
Third Class 4d.

Appendix One

Extract from *The Engineer*, 13th April, 1883

At the beginning of Chapter Two we make reference to an article in *The Engineer* for 13th April, 1883, describing the difficulties, in civil engineering terms, of ensuring that the railway line emerged successfully from Valletta on its journey to Imtarfa (Museum).

The following are extracts from that article and serves further to explain the complexity of the problem facing Messrs Wells-Owen and G. Elwes, civil engineers, of Westminster.

Of the total population of Malta, about 100,000 are directly served by the railway, or about 16,000 per mile of line. Valletta proper is situated on a high narrow tongue of land which divides the Grand Harbour from the Quarantine Harbour. An imposing rampart and ditch separate Valletta from the suburb of Floriana, which lies at the root of the tongue. Outside Floriana is another line of rampart and ditch, which cuts off the communication with the mainland. As the High Street - Strada Reale - of Valletta is the centre of all life, business, and amusement in Malta, it was essential to place the terminus of the railway there, opposite the Opera House.

Military and topographical conditions alike required that the level of the rails at the terminus should be some 35 ft below the level of the street, hence it was necessary to design an underground terminus. The booking office and waiting rooms are on the street level, whence steps conduct to the underground platforms. These last are lighted partly by gas, and partly in the daytime by the light from the end of the tunnel station, which opens on the escarp of the main ditch of Valletta, probably the most imposing military obstacle to assault in all Europe.

The main ditch is crossed by a timber viaduct of four spans of 22 ft 6 in. each, and one of 38 ft, at the end of which - that is, at the counterscarp of the main ditch - the line becomes single, and enters another tunnel 913 yards in length, by which it is conducted through and under the succession of fortifications lying between the main ditch and the outside of Floriana. The tunnel is ventilated at frequent intervals by the shafts which were used for its construction. The alignment of the tunnel was settled after much consideration, in order to meet, as far as possible, the requirements of the military and civil authorities, which was no easy matter, a tunnel directly through the outworks of an important fortress being almost unprecedented. It was subsequently discovered that an ancient subterranean reservoir - the position of which had not been previously known - would be intersected by the proposed line. In order to avoid this reservoir without altering the general alignment of the tunnel, it was decided to go round it, and so the tunnel has the rare feature of a double S curve in the middle of it. The delicate operation of setting out this peculiar alignment underground was successfully accomplished by the resident engineer, so that the headings met, with a difference of about 1 in. only. At half a mile from the terminus there is a second underground station for Floriana. At this point the rails are about 90 ft below the surface of the ground. The long stairs necessary to reach the platform are arranged so as to make the descent and ascent as easy as possible. The line here is single, and space for the platform is provided by increasing the span of the arch forming the roof of the tunnel on one side only. At 47 chains the line crosses a ditch and enters a short tunnel 33 yards long, crosses a second ditch, cuts through the counterscarp, and at 54 chains emerges on the glacis of the outer fortifications. The tunnel is constructed on a falling gradient - towards Notabile - of 1 in 72. Thence to 3¼ miles the gradients are generally level, but from 3¼ miles to the end of the line is almost a continuous ascent, beginning at 1 in 66, increasing to 1 in 50 for the greater part of the distance and terminating by a short piece of 1 in 40 up to the entrance of the Notabile terminus, which is level.

Timetables

The timetable at the opening of the railway, February 1883

TRENI CHE PARTANO

Notabile	San Salvatore	Attard	San Antonio	Birchircara	Msida	Hamrun	Valletta
am	*am*	*am*	*am*	*am*	*am*	*am*	*am*
5.13	5.19	5.25	5.30	5.34	5.38	5.42	5.50
						6.15	6.22
7.12	7.18	7.24	7.29	7.33	7.37	7.41	7.49
10.12	10.18	10.24	10.29	10.33	10.37	10.41	10.49
pm	*pm*	*pm*	*pm*	*pm*	*pm*	*pm*	*pm*
12.12	12.18	12.24	12.29	12.33	12.37	12.41	12.49
2.12	2.18	2.24	2.29	2.33	2.37	2.41	2.49
4.12	4.18	4.24	4.29	4.33	4.37	4.41	4.49
6.12	6.18	6.24	6.29	6.33	6.37	6.41	6.49
7.12			*Treni vucti*			8.06	

TRENI CHE SCENDANO

Valletta	Hamrun	Msida	Birchircara	San Antonio	Attard	San Salvatore	Notabile
am	*am*	*am*	*am*	*am*	*am*	*am*	*am*
5.58	6.05						
6.30	6.38	6.42	6.46	6.50	6.55	7.01	7.07
8.00	8.08	8.12	8.16	8.20	8.25	8.31	8.37
11.00	11.08	11.12	11.16	11.20	11.25	11.31	11.37
pm	*pm*	*pm*	*pm*	*pm*	*pm*	*pm*	*pm*
1.00	1.08	1.12	1.16	1.20	1.25	1.31	1.37
3.00	3.08	3.12	3.16	3.20	3.25	3.31	3.37
5.00	5.08	5.12	5.16	5.20	5.25	5.31	5.37
7.00	7.08	7.12	7.16	7.20	7.25	7.31	7.37

MALTA RAILWAY.

Train Service on and after Monday, 21st April, 1924, and until further notice.

WEEK DAYS

VALLETTA — NOTABILE.

Valletta a.m.	Hamrun a.m.	Birchircara a.m.	Attard a.m.	Notabile (Museum Station) a.m.
§* 4. 30	4. 36	4. 40	5. 0	
§ 5. 46	5. 52	To Birchircara only		
§ 6. 2	6. 7	6. 13	6. 17	6. 37
§ 6. 20	6. 25	6. 32	To Birchircara only	
§ 7. 8	7. 18	7. 25	To Birchircara only	
7. 30	7. 35	7. 41	7. 45	8. 5
§ 7. 50	7. 55	8. 3	To Birchircara only	
8. 35	8. 41	8. 48	8. 52	9. 10
9. 30	9. 35	9. 43	9. 47	10. 5
10. 40	10. 45	10. 54	To Birchircara only	
11. 15	11. 20	11. 29	11. 33	11. 50
p.m.	p.m.	p.m.	p.m.	p.m.
12. 10	12. 15	12. 24	12. 28	12. 45
* 12. 40	12. 45	To Hamrun only		
† 1. 30	1. 35	1. 43	1. 47	2. 5
2. 20	2. 25	2. 33	2. 37	2. 55
3. 10	3. 15	3. 23	3. 27	3. 45
† 4. 10	4. 15	4. 23	4. 27	4. 45
† 5. 10	5. 15	5. 23	5. 27	5. 45
§a5. 30	5. 35	5 43	To Birchircara only	
a 6. 10	6. 15	6. 23	6. 27	6. 45
§a6. 25	6. 31	6. 39	To Birchircara only	
a 7. 10	7. 15	7. 23	7. 27	7. 45
7. 40	7. 45	} To Hamrun only		
8. 30	8. 35			

NOTABILE — VALLETTA.

Notabile (Museum Station) a.m.	Attard a.m.	Birchircara a.m.	Hamrun a.m.	Valletta a.m.
§●a5. 20	5. 32	5. 36	5. 46	5. 50
		§a 6. 0	6. 7	6. 12
		§ 6. 40	6. 47	6. 52
§† 6. 50	7. 2	7. 11	7. 18	7. 23
		§ 7. 28	7. 35	7. 40
		§ 8. 10	8. 18	8. 23
§ 8. 15	8. 29	8. 33	8. 41	8. 46
9. 25	9. 39	9. 43	9. 50	9. 55
10. 18	10. 34	10. 38	10. 45	10. 50
		11. 0	11. 20	11. 25
p.m.	p.m.	p.m.	p.m.	p.m.
12. 5	12. 18	12. 24	12. 32	12. 37
†12. 55	1. 8	1. 12	1. 20	1. 25
			2. 5	2. 10
2. 15	2. 29	2. 33	2. 41	2. 45
† 3. 5	3. 19	3. 23	3. 31	3. 36
4. 5	4. 19	4. 23	4. 31	4. 36
			§ 5 15	5. 20
5. 5	5. 19	5. 23	5. 31	5. 36
		§ 6. 5	6. 15	6. 20
6. 5	6. 19	6. 23	6. 31	6. 36
		§ 6. 45	6. 55	To Hamrun
7. 5	7. 19	7. 23	7. 31	7. 36
7. 55	8. 9	8. 13	8. 21	8. 26

SUNDAYS and FESTIVALS

a.m.	a.m.	a.m.	a.m.	a.m.	a.m.	a.m.	a.m.	a.m.	a.m.
								6. 50	6. 55
7. 0	7. 6	7. 15	7. 18	7. 35	7. 45	7. 57	8. 1	8. 9	8. 15
9. 0	9. 6	9. 15	9. 18	9. 35	9. 45	9. 57	10. 1	10. 9	10. 15
10. 25	10. 30	10. 39	To Birchircara only				10. 42	10. 50	10. 56
							p.m.	p.m.	p.m.
11. 0	11. 6	11. 15	11. 18	11. 35	11. 45	11. 57	12. 1	12. 9	12. 15
p.m.	p.m.	p.m.	p.m.	p.m.	p.m	p.m.			
12. 20	12. 25	To Hamrun only					§§ 1. 0	1. 5	
							1. 55	2. 0	
§§ 1. 15	1. 20	1. 29	1. 33	1. 50	§§ 2. 5	2. 17	2. 23	2. 30	2. 35
2. 10	2. 15	2. 23	2. 27	2. 45	3. 5	3. 17	3. 23	3. 30	3. 35
3. 10	3. 15	3. 23	3. 27	3. 45	4. 5	4. 17	4. 23	4. 30	4. 35
4. 10	4. 15	4. 23	4. 27	4. 45	5. 5	5. 17	5. 23	5. 30	5. 35
5. 10	5. 15	5. 23	5. 27	5. 45	6. 5	6. 17	6. 23	6. 30	6. 35
6. 10	6. 15	6. 23	6. 27	6. 45	● 7. 5	7. 19	7. 23	7. 31	7. 36
7. 10	7. 15	7. 23	7. 27	7. 45	● 7. 55	8. 9	8. 13	8. 21	8. 26
7. 40	7. 45	} To Hamrun only							
8. 30	8 35								

(a). WORKMEN'S TRAIN—The 5.20 a.m. train starts from Notabile and not from Museum Station.
● This train does not stop at San Salvator Station. All other trains only stop at San Salvator Station at the request of passengers
† This train stops at Balzan Station at the request of passengers.
§ No 1st Class accommodation will be provided on this train.
* This train proceeds to Birchircara on Saturdays. No 1st Class accommodation will be provided—Fare 1d.
§§ This train will be suspended after the 29th May.

FARES:—   3rd CLASS
From Valletta to Hamrun	or viceversa	1d.
do. Valletta to Birchircara	do.	2d.
do. Valletta to Attard	do.	3d.
do. Valletta to Museum	do.	4d.
do. Hamrun to Birchircara	do.	1d.
do. Hamrun to Attard	do.	2d.
do. Hamrun to Museum	do.	3d.
do. Birchircara to Attard	do.	1d.
do. Birchircara to Museum	do.	2d.
do. Attard to Museum	do.	1d.

FARES:—   1st CLASS
Between Valletta and Birchircara or any intermediate point 4d.
From Valletta to Attard or viceversa - - - - - - - 6d.
Between Birchircara and Museum or any intermediate point 4d.
From Valletta to Museum or viceversa - - - - - - - 8d.

FARES:—   For Workmen on trains marked (a)
Between Valletta and Birchircara or any intermediate point 1d.
Between Birchircara and Museum or any intermediate point 1d.
From Valletta or Hamrun to Attard or Museum or viceversa 2d.

VALLETTA STATION,
16th April, 1924.

N. BUHAGIAR,
Manager and Engineer.

(181.)   [Price 1d.]

Appendix Three

Managers

Under private ownership

Frank A. B. Geneste	1883-1889 (also a Director)
George Buchanan	1889-1890 (also a Director)
J.C. Gilbert	1890-1891 (also a Director)

Under Government Control

Lawrence Gatt	1892-1896
Nicholas Buhagiar	1897-1924
Carmel Rizzo	1924-1931

The Hon. L. Gatt, CMG, CE

The career of Lawrence Gatt, first Manager of the Malta Railway under Government control, illustrates the policy of considering the appointment to be one available to Government engineers in general, as part of a normal career. Locomotive engineers as such were never recruited. Gatt was born in 1857, and after attending the University of Malta and further education in England, he entered Government service as a land surveyor in 1883. In 1884 he was appointed a railway inspector (the line being then in private hands), in 1885 he became an assistant engineer in the Water Department, 1888 a surveyor in the Public Works Department and in 1892 took up the appointment of Manager of the railway upon its re-opening. Some of his previous appointments had obviously appraised him of the situation and problems of the railway. In 1896 he became chief engineer of water supply and in 1897 Superintendent of Public Works with a seat on the Executive Council and in the Legislative Council. He was created CMG in 1901.

Mr Nicholas Buhagiar examines the trackwork at Museum station, view looking towards Mdina tunnel and Valletta.

The tunnel entrance at Valletta station viewed from the road above in 2004. The Yellow Garage has been established in the tunnel.

Major D. Murray-Bligh

Appendix Four

Exploring the Remains of the Malta Railway
by Roger Cleaver

Whilst wondering where to spend Christmas 1995 in the sun I came across a reference to the defunct Malta Railway which rather caught my interest having spent a fortnight's holiday some 20 or 30 years earlier, touring the island quite intensively on a motorcycle, without ever realising it had once boasted a railway and never noticing any relics of an obviously railway character. I decided 'to kill two birds with one stone' and holiday in Malta and do some railway rambling/exploring as well.

After failing to get any joy from the local libraries, my request in *Railway Ramblings** for information on the Malta Railway brought an excellent response and I was able to piece together the story of this little railway and its route, also the remains still to be found.

My explorations began at Valletta where the original station still exists as the 'Yellow Garage' in a 200 ft-long tunnel in the sandstone beneath Freedom Square by Porta Reale Gate into the city adjacent to the bus station at the inland end of Republic Street, near the ruined Opera House. There once stood a surface station in classical style with Doric columns and framed with a stone pediment, entrances giving access to administrative offices and the booking office and to two ramps downwards towards the 180 ft-long and 15 ft-wide platforms, the station having two tracks with a crossover.

The platform extended out of the tunnel on a viaduct over a defensive ditch between the inner and outer fortifications and passed into a further tunnel (now blocked off) through the ramparts where the two tracks became single, as it was all along the line except for sidings and stations. I found a staircase marked 'Yellow Garage' in the corner of Freedom Square and emerged beside the station tunnel from the end of one of the original ramp tunnels, where I located the present owner who was quite happy to let me wander round on my own and told me it had been a garage since 1971. He put on the lights in the second foot ramp/tunnel that emerges into the garage itself, the floor being ridged for grip and the tunnel now blocked off about 50 ft in.

The viaduct outside the station is still in place but as the further tunnel was blocked it was necessary to walk through the bus station and ahead into Floriana to find the surface building of Floriana station, which is still there, unrecognisable as a station, as it always was, and used by the 'Agrikultura' (whatever that might be) as offices. The stairway down to the 90 ft deep platforms in the tunnel below is now blocked off and the building stands in a quiet corner behind the Methodist church and adjacent to the Argotti Gardens some 850 yds from Valletta station. The Floriana tunnel was used as an air raid shelter during World War II but now carries cables and conduits.

The rails emerged at St Phillip's Bastion, crossed the roadway and went through yet another bastion, the 'Fausse Bray', both entrances now blocked, emerging to cross a dry defensive ditch on a little five-arched stone bridge which is still *in situ* and very easily accessible, then crossed a patch of rough ground with stunted trees in a shadow cutting now filled. At this point, due to road development, widening and new cuttings and urban development, the railway has been eradicated right up to Hamrun station.

Originally, after crossing the rough strip of land the railway passed over the Princess Melita Road on a girder bridge preceded by a stone arch over the tree-lined pavement to run on straight almost parallel to the Blata il Baida Road on the left. At about one mile from Valletta the line swung from south-west to west for another half mile before reaching Hamrun station.

* A version of this account was subsequently published in *Railway Ramblings*, the journal of the Railway Ramblers, in 2001, and is reproduced here by kind permission.

The tunnel entrance at Valletta in 2004, now the Yellow Garage.   *Major D. Murray-Bligh*

Former viaduct across outer defensive ditch at Porte des Bombes near Floriana in 1998.
                A.M. Lawrence

I tried without success to trace the route up to Hamrun, where some early references mention a run through open country and small fields, now a densely populated suburb. For anyone following in my footsteps, don't be afraid to ask directions of the locals. Maltese people are so friendly and helpful and often more knowledgeable about their old railway, gone over 60 years, than many a local in an English village about a main line gone only 20 or 30 years!

Hamrun station is still standing and lies about 100 yards off the main road through Hamrun, down a side road called Triq il Ferrovia (literally Street of the Iron Road), the police station, the rail station lying on the right-hand side where the road splits three ways at a tree-covered island and is inside a yard fronting the street with two big metal gates and stands complete with its canopy as the Hamrun Boy Scouts headquarters. Hamrun was the engineering headquarters with lines leading off to sheds and workshops, under a lush background of trees, the workshops being taken over by a milk processing and distribution company some years ago.

The route on to Msida from here I was not able to trace due to much altered road layouts, differences in ground levels, new cuts and infills all serving to confuse. However, the general direction can be followed as leaving Hamrun the line turned on a sharpish curve to run slightly west of north for about a half mile and about 300 yds before Msida station it rose onto an embankment, neither of which remains. Msida was never more than a small Halt of an earth platform edged with stones, so there never was much to remain anyway. There followed Santa Venera, which may or may not have been an official Halt, or more simply a place near Santa Venera where the train would stop if asked. In fact, trains may have stopped anywhere on the line if hailed by an intending passenger!

On reaching Birkirkara, the line once more at ground level, having run out of the middle of Psaila Street and across Fleur-de-Lys Road, ran across a small square, now the town bus terminal, at 2 miles 1,658 yds, through a pair of imposing iron gates, flanked by pedestrian gates, into the lush tree-lined garden that was Birkirkara station (*see overleaf*). The gates are still there, as are the gardens, Nicholas Buhagiar's circular fountain, and best of all, the station building complete and unaltered externally with its canopy and benches and even the station name over the door. Opposite stands a restored passenger carriage minus the wheels, balcony-ended and louvre-windowed with longitudinal bench seating, built I believe of teak and painted in the red to which they had to resort as the summer sun was more than a match for the varnish originally used.

Behind the station a dignified two-storey stone building with side balconies, used now as local council offices, is a lovely old set of steps through a gated arch leading into a quiet side street, leading in turn into the main street. This is a delightful place to sit in the shade among the flowers in the spring-like warmth and sunshine I encountered over the Christmas period.

The aforementioned Nicholas Buhagiar, a most enterprising and imaginative manager, who seemed to have a great deal of pride in 'his' railway, had the brilliant idea of using catchment pits lined with rubble and trenches lined with chippings to catch the run-off of water from the tracks and adjacent roads to irrigate this oasis of orange and lemon trees, palms and carobs. Oh, to sit there then with your cronies in the blue twilight of a Mediterranean summer evening, your pipe in one hand and a glass of wine or a cool beer in the other, listening to the clank of the rods and the squeal of flanges on the guard-rail, the chuff of the tank engine and the smell of smoke, steam and hot oil as the evening train brings in old chums to join your circle, and perhaps a few strange faces, to be wondered at and discussed long after they've departed into the gathering dusk.

The railway left by a gate at the far end of its garden, next to the overlooking church, and ran straight ahead along what is now a residential back road, past the site of Balzan station (of which there is now no trace), totally submerged by houses flanking the road at 3 miles 570 yards. This was a little stone-bound earth Halt on a lane which connected the two east-west roads, Strada Reale and Strada Sant' Antonio, which parallel the line at this point.

The preserved carriage in the public garden at Birkirkara station in 2004. The garden was formally opened by the Hon. Eddie Fenech Adami, the Maltese Prime Minister, on 26th August, 1992.   *Major D. Murray-Bligh*

Birkirkara station entrance viewed from the east side in 2004.   *Major D. Murray-Bligh*

The steps to the eastern side of Birkirkara station entrance in 2004.   *Major D. Murray-Bligh*

A general view along the site of the former Birkirkara station platform in 2004 showing the well-maintained gardens.

Major D. Murray-Bligh

At a further 330 yards was San Anton Halt with palm and tamarisk trees on a further lane connecting the two lateral roads already mentioned. This lane is now a short (300 yard) dual-carriageway with lush palms on a central median, leading down to the very beautiful San Anton Palace and gardens, the home of the Maltese Premier and an idyllic spot to while away an afternoon checking out the many species of trees and plants, viewing the many cage-birds or even trying to cheer up the resident camel who always seems to have the hump.

As a point of interest, if you walk down the right-hand pavement as you approach the short dual-carriageway and site of San Anton Halt, count back three trees from the junction. The first two are tall palms and the third is a quite substantial noon-palm-type tree on a raised bed about 12 ft in diameter. You will see on the pavement side of the tree, protruding from the earth is a 4 ft length of light flat-bottomed rail, drilled at the end for a fish-plate, and partially grown around by the tree trunk. This was the only piece of rail I saw on my exploration, and wonder if it was lifted from its original location a few yards away after closure of the line and then hammered into the ground to support what was then a scrawny sapling?

Immediately across the dual-carriageway is a very tangible relic, the start of an embankment of 50 yards to the site of Attard station. This starts at ground level and climbs to about 12 foot high, about eight ft wide at the top, walled by sloping sides of limestone blocks and is easily walked on the short grass top, soon coming to the stone butresses of the now removed girder bridge over the Attard-Birkirkara road, which once had a central support column, now also gone.

Another 100 yds or so brought me to the site of Attard station, now a children's playground, but with the central track position marker with a strip of light-coloured brick, where all else is reddish-brick. The disappeared station building is also marked out with yellow brick to show the front openings, solid walls, etc. The ticket office, a 10 ft square stone building, is still extant a few yards away by the road. This was a spacious tree-lined station with its circular flower beds giving shade and colour for passengers.

On leaving, the line crossed the busy Strada San Antonio to enter a substantial rock cutting about ½ mile-long to cross the Ta Kali Road on the level after rising up from its 14 ft depth. A 1960 report says there was a bridge standing, 300 yards up the cutting, that carried a minor road over. Well, the cutting has now been filled and is lined with houses and there is no sign of the bridge although the new road is called Triq il Linja, Line Road.

All these crossing points over roads were controlled by 'catenas', who had a little stone guard-hut, and placed a chain across the road on both sides of the line to prevent traffic, then mostly horses and carts from crossing the line; and then across the track on the passing of a train as there were no level crossing gates. Many were the incidents of horses running into the chains or engines carrying carrying the chains away on their buffer beams!

The major road crossing at Valletta/Floriana was, as previously mentioned, on a bridge, as was the crossing outside Attard, but at ground level road crossings at Birkirkara and Attard stations the trains were seen over the road by the station staff. Minor country lane crossings were not guarded at all.

After crossing Ta Kali Road there is about 100 yards of low 18 in. embankment remaining before this disappears under later housing all the way up to the site of San Salvatore station, on the corner with Rabat Road, 'Via Notabile', at 4 miles 1,200 yards, having crossed a small four-arched bridge, no longer standing, over a little stream. The station had one platform, but none of the luxuriant floral display of other stations, although palm trees were planted. There was a bridge here carrying the Via Notabile over the line, but this, with the cutting and the station, once used by visitors, staff and patients at the nearby mental hospital, have all disappeared, as has the first 100 yards of trackbed beyond the road, across small fields of cabbages, lemon trees, etc.

A view looking away from the site of Attard station towards Valletta (*see page 42*) in 2004.
Major D. Murray-Bligh

A cast-iron sign at Attard mounted on piece of rail in 2004 (*see page 43*). *Major D. Murray-Bligh*

THESE CAROB TREES, GROWN FROM SEED SOWN AT TA XBIEX VILLA NURSERY IN 1893, WERE TRANSPLANTED IN THIS STATION (ATTARD) IN 1897

By skirting around to the left and then paralleling the line on a sandy track by the hospital wall, I could see where the five foot high stone-sided embankment emerged again from a cultivated field over to my right and by walking up the edge of a field I was able to regain the line, now used as an access track to the little fields, and followed it out to a busy main road with a central dividing hedge at which point it was not possible to progress further due to lack of access, private property, unfriendly dogs and a lack of visible remains. So I turned right and walked up to the roundabout below Mdina where the Via Notabile joins and a short walk to the left brought me in line with the moat by the vast bastion to the left above me. I followed a block-ended road back for 200-300 yards to find what I believe was the surface building of Notabile station, and by skirting around to the right behind this I found the end-infilled cutting leading into the blocked-up mouth of the tunnel that ran half a mile under Mdina to emerge just before Museum station. Notabile platforms at rail level are now buried some 20-30 feet under a small field.

I walked back up the rising road towards Mdina, and after crossing the main road, went up the steps opposite which brought me up to a square on my right, where a left and right turn took me along Museum Road in Rabat, opposite the citadel walls of Mdina on my right, and then right again along Museum Boulevard to just short of the Museum of Roman Antiquities. Here I took the tree-lined station approach road on my right downhill, at first parallel to the railway and then round a right bend, and arrived at Museum station situated about 100 yards from the exit portal of Notabile tunnel. With its date of construction in the key stone of the arch, and now blocked by a wall with a door in it and used either for storage or to grow mushrooms, so a local dog-walker informed me, but as nobody was around in the wired off area in front of the portal and there are no signs to indicate usage, I cannot be sure.

Museum station, at 6 miles 1,600 yards was once a derelict eyesore, but has been restored as the 'Station Restaurant' with the platform area beneath the old canopy glassed-in for dining. The owner was very amenable to my having a look around, this being mid-morning and no customers were on the premises. The interior is spacious, light and cool with the dressed stone walls lined with large sepia photographs of the railway in its heyday, including Museum station and long-dead moustachioed worthies posing proudly in bright sunlight beside their engines, or outside the station where they were employed.

Outside the station, in front, stands one of Mr Buhagiar's circular flower beds with a fountain, no longer working, in the centre. This makes a handy turn-around for vehicles as well as being a pleasant feature. There was a loop line here at Museum, allowing an engine to run-round its train, but no turntable or triangle on the line meant that engines could not be turned.

I walked on along the 400 yard embankment beyond the station, now another approach road, crossing a very substantial original stone bridge over a small stream about 50 ft below in a valley, the route still lined by the original cruciform concrete fencing up to the end, originally at the brick wall at the foot of the hill below Imtarfa barracks, now a rather tatty dual carriageway junction, at a final 7 miles 240 yds.

If any rambler is intending to visit Malta and explore the railway, I would suggest they take their walking boots. Some of the terrain is pretty rough and that they go, if possible, in the autumn or winter season when the spring-like weather is more conducive to walking and scrambling about.

A recent view of the station at Museum.

Museum station in 2003 looking towards the viaduct and the end of the line.   *A.M. Lawrence*

Sources and Bibliography

Bradshaw's Railway Manual: Shareholders' Guide and Directory 1885. Item 326. Malta Railway Co. Ltd.

Busuttil, V., *A Tourist's Guide to the Maltese Islands, Malta Herald*, 1916.

Bryans, Robin, *Malta and Gozo*, Faber and Faber, 1966.

Bradford, E., *The Great Siege, Malta 1565*, Penguin Books, 1964.

Bloom, U., *Down to the Sea in Ships*, Hutchinson, 1958.

Blouet, B., *The Story of Malta*, Faber, 1967.

Bowen-Jones, Dewdney and Fisher, *Malta: Background for Development*, Department of Geography, University of Durham, 1961.

Castagna, P.P., *History of Malta* (in Italian), 1893.

Collingbridge, W.H. & L., *Malta and Gibraltar Illustrated*, 1915.

Crotchet, 'Malta's Vanished Tramways', *Times of Malta*, 28th January, 1963.

Crotchet, Malta's Railway', *Times of Malta*, 19th February, 1963.

The Engineer, 1883.

Gatt, L., *Report on the management and working of the Malta Railway from 25th February, 1892, to 24th February, 1893*, printed by J. Muscat.

Government of Malta, Department of Information. Notes on Archbishop Scicluna.

Hogg, G., *Malta, Blue-Water Island*, Allen & Unwin, 1967.

Hughes, Quentin, *Works on Architecture in Malta (1968-1973).*

The Locomotive 1927. 'The Malta Railway' by A.R. Bennett MILE

The *Railway Magazine*, 1912. 'The Malta Railway' by F.S.W.

    1929. 'Malta Railway', by F.M.

    1934. 'Closing of the Malta Railway', by A.S. Coase.

    1941. 'The Derelict Malta Railway'.

Malta newspapers for 3rd March, 1883. Report of the opening of the railway and various subsequent reports and articles.

Melitensia Collection, The Royal Malta Library. Annual Reports submitted to Government by the Manager of the Railway Department.

Parke, J.F., 'Bus Services in Malta', Omnibus Society, Undated.

Patent Office, Patent taken out by L. Bissel, 1857. The Bissel Truck.

Public Record Office:

    File BT 31/2535/13145. The Malta Railway Company.

    File BT 31/2220/10479. The Valletta-Notabile Railway Co.

Pearce, F.R.G., *Illustrated Guide to Historic Malta*, 1961.

Robins, Bryan, *Malta and Gozo*, Faber & Faber, 1966.

Swann, J.E., 'Retracing the Malta Railway', *Times of Malta*, May/June 1965.

Taylor, G.C., 'Journal of adventures with the British Army from the commencement of the War to the taking of Sevastopol - 1856'.

Vignoles, O.J., *Life of C.B. Vignoles*, Longmans, Green, 1889.

Zammitt, E.N., 'The formal opening of the Malta Railway, 1883' (in Italian).

Acknowledgements

I am most grateful to the following who have given their time, enthusiasm and knowledge in research and the identification of sources and documents. In particular I thank Professor J. Galea, MBE, MD, The Royal University of Malta; Dr K. Graham, lately a regular passenger, Malta Railway; and J.E. Swann, B.Sc., C.Eng., MIE, lately Lecturer at the Malta College of Arts, Science and Technology whose encouragement and help have extended over some years.

A. Andrews, Archivist, Birmingham Public Libraries; E. Atkinson, Archivist, British Transport Historical Records; Miss W. Buhagiar (daughter of Nicholas Buhagiar, Manager, Malta Railway, 1897-1924); C. Cassar, Chief Draughtsman, Office of Public Works, Malta; L. Cliff, The Hunslet Engine Co. Ltd; Dr V.A. Depasquale, LL.D, Librarian, The Royal Malta Library; E.J. Farrugia, lately driver, The Malta Railway; A. Zammit Gabarritta, Research Officer, The Royal Malta Library; Mr J.W. Gatt; Richard L. Hills, Department of History of Science and Technology, University of Manchester; G. Horsman; Messrs Hunslet (Holdings) Co. Ltd.; D.W. King, OBE, Chief Librarian, The Ministry of Defence Library (Central and Army); Alistair B. McLeod; Members of the staff of *The Times of Malta*; H. Milligan, The Manchester Public Libraries; G. Ottley, FLA, The British Museum State Paper Room; P.J. Parkinson, Directorate of Military Survey; R.F. Roberts. Hon. Librarian, The Stephenson Locomotive Society; A. Raimondo, C.Eng., MIEE, Headmaster, Paola Technical Institute, Malta; H. Smedley and G. Arnott, Traction Division, The English Electric Company Ltd; Cyril Smith, The Railway Correspondence & Travel Society; Dominic V. Stellin, lately Senior Apprentice, The Malta Railway; Major M.C. Sacco, MBE, Royal Malta Artillery; L.A. Sornet, Metropolitan-Cammell Ltd; The Hon. Mabel Strickland, OBE; Mr A. Pisani, President, Malta Hobbies Society; Mrs E. Thomas, FLA, Chief Librarian, Army Western Command; J.G. Tennent, MPS, the Omnibus Society; W.A. Taylor, MC, FLA, City Librarian, Birmingham; E. Vassallo, Senior Assistant Secretary, Office of Public Works, Valletta; C.G. Zammitt, FSA, Director, The National Museum, Valletta, Malta.

In 1995 I received a letter from Mr A.V. Gera, enclosing the splendid photograph which is reproduced on page 64 and on the front cover. Major D. Murray-Bligh originated the illustrations of the locomotives featured on the cover and assisted by locating and photographing existing relics of the railway.

Anyone who has an affection for Malta and its citizens (and there must be an enormous number of such) will be aware of the important contribution to the history of Malta made by the firm of R. Ellis, photographers, of Kingsway, Valletta. The high quality of their work is self-evident.

The *Railway Magazine* for permission to quote from the several articles mentioned. Messrs Hunslet (Holdings) Ltd for going to much trouble to discover drawings and photographs of Nos. 1, 5 and 6 and for permission to use them. The English Electric Co. Ltd (Vulcan Works) for similarly undertaking much research work to produce dimensions and catalogue print of No. 4 and for permission to use these. The Birmingham City Library for the general arrangement drawings of the Cammell-Laird rolling stock and for permission to use them. The University of Manchester Institute of Science and Technology for the general arrangement drawings of the Beyer, Peacock locomotives and for their permission to use them. The Omnibus Society for permission to quote from a paper on the bus services of Malta. The Ministry of Defence Library for material on George Cavendish Taylor. The Royal Malta Library for permission to quote from the Melitensia Collection, the annual reports of the Railway Manager.

Transcripts of Crown copyright records in the Public Record Office appear by permission of the Controller HM Stationery Office. Messrs Ian Allan Ltd, proprietors of the Locomotive Publishing Co. Ltd, for permission to quote from the article by A.R. Bennett in *The Locomotive* 1927, and a paper produced by the Omnibus Society. *The Times of Malta* for permission to quote from various articles which have appeared in that newspaper. The staff of Chester Public Library for much help in general research. *The Engineer*, for permission to quote from the 1883 edition. The Office of Public Works, Malta, for much help with maps and plans.

Our final view is of the site of Attard station in 2004, now a children's playground. The site's past has not been completely forgotten. Could that be a representation of Black, Hawthorn 0-6-0 locomotive No. 4 for the local children to play on! *Major D. Murray-Bligh*

Index